Classroom Insights From Educational Psychology

A Developmental Approach to Educating Young Children

Denise H. Daniels • Patricia K. Clarkson

A Joint Publication

CORWIN
A SAGE Company

Division 15: Educational Psychology
American Psychological Association

KH

For information:

Corwin
A SAGE Company
2455 Teller Road
Thousand Oaks, California 91320
(800) 233-9936
Fax: (800) 417-2466
www.corwin.com

SAGE Ltd.
1 Oliver's Yard
55 City Road
London EC1Y 1SP
United Kingdom

SAGE India Pvt. Ltd.
B 1/I 1 Mohan Cooperative
   Industrial Area
Mathura Road, New Delhi 110 044
India

SAGE Asia-Pacific Pte. Ltd.
33 Pekin Street #02-01
Far East Square
Singapore 048763

Printed in the United States of America

Library of Congress Cataloging-in-Publication Data

Daniels, Denise H. (Denise Honeycutt), 1960-
A developmental approach to educating young children / Denise H. Daniels, Patricia K. Clarkson.
   p. cm. — (Classroom insights from educational psychology)
Includes bibliographical references and index.
ISBN 978-1-4129-8114-9 (pbk.)
1. Early childhood education. 2. Child development. I. Clarkson, Patricia K. II. Title.
   III. Series.

LB1139.23.D35 2010
372.21—dc22   2010020320

This book is printed on acid-free paper.

10   11   12   13   14   10   9   8   7   6   5   4   3   2   1

Acquisitions Editor:	Jessica Allan
Associate Editor:	Joanna Coelho
Editorial Assistant:	Allison Scott
Production Editor:	Amy Schroller
Copy Editor:	Tina Hardy
Typesetter:	C&M Digitals (P) Ltd.
Proofreader:	Victoria Reed-Castro
Indexer:	Sheila Bodell
Cover Designer:	Anthony Paular

1/21/11

Contents

Series Preface to *Classroom Insights*   v
Barbara L. McCombs and Debra K. Meyer

Acknowledgments   viii

About the Authors   ix

Introduction   1

Chapter 1. Developmental Perspectives and Educational Practice   7
Viewing Children and Teachers in the Big Picture
    Ecological Perspective   9
    The Developmental Shift From Early
       to Middle Childhood   11
    Teachers' Perspectives on Development
       and Practice   24

Chapter 2. Early School Adjustment   31
Fostering Children's Adjustment and Self-Regulation
    Early School Adjustment Models   33
    Readiness of the Child   35
    Readiness of the Teacher   45
    Children at Risk for Adjustment Difficulties   49
    Readiness of the School   57
    Children's Views of School   60

Chapter 3. The Primacy of Relationships in the Early School Years   65
Fostering Relationships
    School Reform Models   67

Teacher-Child Relationships   69
Child-Child Relationships in School   78
Teacher-Parent Relationships and
    Family Involvement in School   84

**Chapter 4. Developmentally Appropriate
  Classroom Practices**   **91**
Fostering Learning in the Classroom
    Social-Constructivist Approaches   95
    Classroom Climate   99
    Classroom Organization   102
    Classroom Instruction   107

**Chapter 5. Children's Learning in Digital
  and Natural Environments**   **115**
Connecting Learning Out of the Classroom
    Educational Technology for Children   118
    Outdoor Education   128

Conclusion   **139**

Resource A. Tools for Reflection and Improvement **143**

**Resource B. Professional Organizations
  and Model Programs**   **173**

Resource C. Recommended Reading   **179**

Glossary   **181**

References   **185**

Index   **193**

Series Preface to *Classroom Insights*

Division 15, *Educational Psychology,* of the American Psychological Association and Corwin have partnered to create the innovative *Classroom Insights From Educational Psychology* series for teachers in an effort to reduce the widening gap between research and theory on learning, teaching, and classroom practice. Educational psychology is a discipline that seeks to understand the integration among human development and learning, classroom learning environments and instructional strategies, and student learning and assessment. In this way, the field of educational psychology is among the most relevant and applicable for teachers.

While on the one hand, we have seen great advances in our understanding of student learning and instructional practices over the last decade, these advances are not highly visible in today's classrooms, pre-service and graduate teacher education programs, or professional development for teachers. Consequently, classroom practice for the most part does not seem to be highly influenced by current research and theory in educational psychology. Yet federal legislation such as the *No Child Left Behind Act of 2001,* state and local agencies, and many school districts and grant programs call for "scientifically-based practices," "research-based methods," or "evidence-based decisions." As part of the solution to this problem, this series of short, easily accessible books for teachers is designed to reflect in-depth, high quality research, to be used in a variety of educational settings, and is endorsed by Division 15.

As the *Classroom Insights* series evolves over the years that new volumes are released, we as editors will continue to work with teachers to identify those topics that are most relevant to their current contexts and goals for student learning. We will also be guided by current and evolving research that honors the best practices of teachers and schools that are making proven efforts to reach all students and to help them succeed in their schooling and in retaining their love of learning. The research and practice knowledge base is honored by our commitment to have every book authored by an educational psychologist and at least one teacher colleague.

The goals of this series are threefold:

- To give practicing and pre-service teachers access to current advances in research and theory on classroom teaching and learning in an easily understood and usable form.
- To align teacher preparation, advanced study, and professional development with current advances in research and theory, which have not been widely shared with teachers.
- To highlight how the most effective teaching practices are based upon a substantial research base and created within classrooms, rather than applied in a "one-size-fits-all" or "silver bullet" approach across classrooms.

Classroom Insights provides a series of specialized books that will improve teaching and learning in PreK–12 classrooms by focusing on what is most important and relevant to today's teachers. In some volumes the applications are limited to specific age levels or characteristics of students, while in others the ideas can be broadly applied across PreK–12 settings. Classroom strategies are integrated throughout every book and each includes a wide array of resources for teachers to use to study their own practices and improve student achievement and classroom learning environments. Finally, many of these research-based applications will be new approaches and frame-works that have never been published in a series for teachers.

As series editors our goal is to provide the most up-to-date professional series of teacher resources for connecting teachers with the best and most relevant research in our field of educational psychology. We have planned for every page to provide useful insights for teachers into their current practices in ways that will help them transform classroom learning for their students, themselves, and their school communities.

Sincerely,
Your Series Editors

Barbara L. McCombs, PhD
Senior Research Scientist
University of Denver

Debra K. Meyer, PhD
Professor
Elmhurst College

Acknowledgments

Corwin gratefully acknowledges the contributions of the following reviewers:

Yolanda Abel
Assistant Professor
School of Education
Johns Hopkins University
Baltimore, MD

Carole S. Campbell
Early Childhood Specialist and Special Educator
Higher Ground Educational Consulting
Green Valley, AZ

Julie Frederick
Kindergarten Teacher
Broadview Thomson Elementary
Seattle, WA

Katina Keener
Science/Social Studies, Grades 1 & 2
T.C. Walker Elementary School
Gloucester, VA

About the Authors

 **Denise H. Daniels** is a professor of child development at California Polytechnic State University at San Luis Obispo and a former associate professor of educational psychology at Northern Illinois University. She received her PhD in Education and Developmental Studies from University of California, Los Angeles in 1992. She draws from nearly 20 years of experience teaching educators and other child professionals at undergraduate and graduate levels. Denise's research focuses on children's adjustment and motivation to learn in school and the development of children's and teachers' psychological understandings and beliefs about education. She is involved in a variety of community and state endeavors to promote high quality early educational practices.

 **Patricia K. Clarkson** is an early education professional who has over 20 years of experience as a director, teacher, and seminar leader. Patty is currently a doctoral candidate in the joint doctoral program in Educational Leadership at University of California, Santa Barbara. She received a BS in Psychology and Human Development and an MA in Education Administration from California Polytechnic University at San

Luis Obispo. Her research interests include teacher beliefs and practices in early childhood education and teacher training programs. Patty has established herself as a leader in early education through developing and directing a private P–6th grade educational program and leading early education seminars in conferences throughout Southern California.

Introduction

The purpose of this book is to provide educators with a friendly introduction to some current ideas from research on child development and education for improving practices in the early school years. These years provide "windows of opportunity" for children to develop attitudes, learning approaches, and competencies essential for their future well-being and achievement in school. In the past two decades, educational and developmental psychologists and others have made great strides in understanding how to launch children onto positive developmental pathways through school (see topic areas in Figure 0.1). We also know more about how to help steer children away from negative pathways. We would like to share these insights with teachers and other child professionals because of the critical role that they play in this endeavor. Of course, others—such as parents, administrators, community members, policymakers—also play important roles, but we primarily focus on what classroom teachers can do to support children's learning and development. It is important to note that most of the recommendations made in this brief book have the typically developing child in mind; however, some attention is given to individual differences.

Objectives

The *Classroom Insights* series was created to help bridge the gap between current theory and research in educational and developmental psychology and classroom practice. The major

Figure 0.1   Promoting Positive Pathways Through School

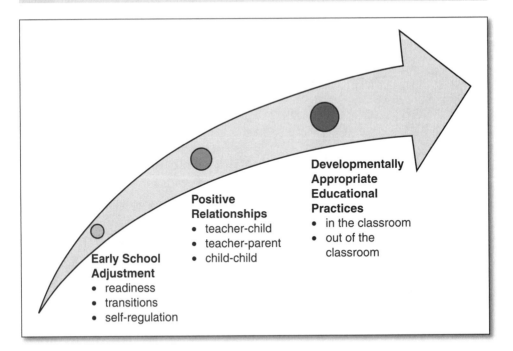

objective of this book is to expose practicing and prospective educators of children in preschool and the primary grades to some current advances in developmental research with implications for classroom practice. We hope teacher educators will also find this source useful. We want to encourage educators to do the following:

- *View children and teachers in the big picture:* Better understand major developmental changes in the child from early to middle childhood, typical changes in school contexts during these years, and how adult beliefs about development impact their interactions with children and the learning environments they create for them. Developmental knowledge is key to improving educational practices.

- *Foster children's adjustment and self-regulation:* Better understand the influence of child and classroom qualities on children's regulatory behaviors and their early school adjustment and how to facilitate smooth transitions to school and between grade levels.
- *Foster relationships:* Better understand the influence of teacher-child, child-child, and teacher-parent relationships on children's development and learning throughout the school years.
- *Foster learning in the classroom:* Better understand the influence of classroom climate, organization, and instructional practices on children's learning and development.
- *Connect learning out of the classroom:* Better understand children's learning and development in digital and natural environments.

Each of these topics is discussed in separate chapters introduced next. Each chapter provides brief background information from current research and theory and recommendations for practice.

OVERVIEW

We begin Chapter 1 with a brief overview of important developmental changes in children's thinking, feelings, behavior, and social relationships between four and eight years—the age range of interest in this book. Children show remarkable growth in all areas of development during these years, simply referred to as "the 5 to 7 developmental shift." In addition, they typically experience multiple changes in their environments, such as transitions to new schools and classrooms and increased expectations at home. Preschool and primary-grade teachers who understand these complex developmental changes from an ecological perspective are better prepared to guide the hearts and minds of children and provide secure and stimulating learning experiences for them.

In Chapter 2, we describe behaviors, skills, and attitudes that children develop in the early school years that appear to be critical for their adjustment and later achievements in school. Particular attention is given to the development of self-regulation skills. This chapter also includes information about how school practices and transitional activities affect children's adjustment. We also refer to some individual differences in children's abilities to adapt to school and provide some recommendations for responding to children who might be at risk for difficulties, such as those with aggressive or inhibited tendencies.

Chapter 3 focuses on the importance of developing positive relationships in school. Teachers' relationships with children not only influence children's current adjustment and learning but their relationships with peers and future teachers as well as subsequent school attitudes and achievement. In addition, teachers' relationships with parents play an important role in fostering family involvement in school and children's long-term adjustment and achievement. Recommendations for fostering positive relationships in school are provided on the basis of this research.

Chapter 4 provides a brief introduction to how young children's learning and development is influenced by the classroom climate, organization, and general instructional practices in preschool and primary grades. This approach is primarily based on social-constructivist perspectives of development, and it includes rationales for including play in school for optimal learning and well-being. Examples of high quality practices are provided. Other books in the *Classroom Insights* series will attend to specific practices and teaching of particular academic subjects.

Chapter 5 includes discussions about how children's experiences with technology and nature influence their learning and development and how teachers might connect to or extend these experiences.

The brief concluding chapter highlights the importance of implementing developmental approaches in the early school years, as well as some of the challenges teachers face and how obstacles might be overcome.

Brief cases or vignettes from the classroom (*Window Into Practice, The Child's Window*) are threaded throughout the text to provide real-life connections and illustrations of the material presented in chapters. In addition, simple guidelines for observations and interviews are included in *Practice Exercises* to help readers connect content to live examples. *Summaries, Questions to Ponder,* and *Key Words* are provided at the end of each chapter for monitoring and enhancing comprehension.

The *Resources* section provides additional reflection tools and resources for prospective and practicing teachers and others. In *Resource A*, recommendations from the text are reproduced for a handy reference and include further suggestions for reflecting upon, improving, and monitoring practices; these can be adapted for a variety of purposes. *Resource B* provides descriptions of and links to major professional organizations and centers for obtaining resources, guides, and materials for implementing developmentally appropriate practices. *Resource C* introduces books with excellent practical suggestions and books with inspiring stories about real children and teachers in preschool and primary-grade classrooms. We hope that connecting developmental research to life in the classroom enlightens all of us with the passion for educating and improving the lives of young children.

1

Developmental Perspectives and Educational Practice

Viewing Children and Teachers in the Big Picture

Window Into Practice

Charlotte was a new first-grade school teacher in an urban school. She was bilingual and looked forward to working with children from diverse backgrounds. She received her multiple subject teaching credential from a respected university; the focus of the program was on building children's literacy skills and family-school connections in the early grades. She knew that she faced a challenge teaching mostly children from lower income households who had little preschool experience and spoke mostly Spanish. The kindergarten teachers told her that only a few children could read words in either English or Spanish, and they expected some would have difficulties adjusting to the longer school day. Charlotte also understood some of the strengths the children brought to the classroom. For example, she expected that most children would have positive attitudes toward school and abilities to cooperate with each other on schoolwork; these approaches were learned within their families. Her first year was tough. Being constantly on alert, preparing lessons, dealing with difficult children and parents, and participating in afterschool events demanded so much time and energy. She was always tired. She was particularly haunted by difficulties with Miguel's aggressive behavior. But she was also satisfied with her progress, particularly because she had formed such positive relationships with her students. They continually shared smiles, hugs, and events with her, even after leaving her classroom. She also saw tremendous growth in children's literacy skills and was quite proud of her success in creating learning stations where small groups of children worked on different assignments while she assisted one group with reading in English and Spanish. One of her unanticipated challenges was teaching math; she realized that she had obtained less education in this area and she had difficulties with creating interesting learning activities for children (few manipulatives were available in the classroom), often resorting to giving children worksheets to work on together. Her mentor pointed out that children were simply providing each other with answers, particularly to subtraction problems—a common difficulty for this age group—so collaborative learning was not effective. With her mentor's assistance, she read a bit more about children's developing mathematical abilities and then ordered and created appropriate math materials, revised lessons, and reorganized the afternoon learning centers. She ended the school year with many new ideas for improving math instructional practices in the future. She also vowed to communicate with parents earlier in the school year, so that she might create positive relationships before she had to discuss difficulties with children. Charlotte also wanted to add suggestions as to how parents might support children's learning at home. She discovered too late that many parents deliberately disengaged from children's reading activities at home because they thought they would interfere with the teacher's instruction. Rosa's mother helped her understand this point of view; simply providing some specific suggestions about what to do would inspire parents to support their children's education.

Charlotte is an example of a teacher with an **ecological perspective** on children's development and learning in school. She considers how to interact with children in terms of their previous experiences at home and in school and communicates with parents and previous teachers. She also expects children to arrive with some common developmental needs and competencies, such as the need for secure relations with teachers, high interests in learning, and emerging abilities to get along with others and control their behavior, as well as some individual differences in their temperaments and academic skills. She creates a semistructured classroom environment with a range of learning activities based on this knowledge. But most of all, she attends to her own interactions with children because she knows that the first-grade transition is difficult, trying to listen carefully to children and show warmth and acceptance toward all.

This chapter establishes the foundation for subsequent chapters by providing a brief introduction to some contemporary perspectives on child development. It begins with a discussion about ecological models of development and general implications for educating young children. Educators with ecological perspectives recognize how children's developing qualities and experiences in different settings influence each other and affect their learning in the classroom. Next, we describe major developments in children's thinking, feeling, and regulated behavior between 4 and 8 years of age and how typical changes in environments for children between these ages might contribute to or hinder their development. (The following chapters look at children's development of thinking processes and relationships in more detail and offer specific recommendations for practice.) Finally, we attend to teacher perspectives on child development and education and how their beliefs influence their interactions with children and classroom practices.

ECOLOGICAL PERSPECTIVE

As biologists study relationships between organisms (plants and animals) and their environments, developmental scientists study children's relationships and interactions with others in multiple environmental contexts (Bronfenbrenner, 1979; Bronfenbrenner & Morris, 1998). From this view depicted in

Figure 1.1, the child at the center of the ecological model is born with particular characteristics (e.g., sex, temperament, mental and physical capabilities) that influence behavior in immediate settings (microsystems), especially home, school, peer groups, and neighborhoods. Developmental scientists also examine connections between the different settings (mesosystems), such as how parents, teachers, and peers relate to one another. Interactions in these multiple settings shape the child's development, and as the child changes, the interactions change. In addition, researchers consider how elements of the broader social and cultural contexts affect these interactions (exo- and macrosystems not shown), for example, how the No Child Left Behind Act influences school practices, and in turn, teacher-child interactions in the classroom.

A major assumption of the ecological model is that these various subsystems change over the course of development. Change can originate within the child, as when a 6-year-old learns to better regulate his behavior, or outside the child, as when there is a school change from preschool to kindergarten.

Figure 1.1   Dynamic Ecological Model

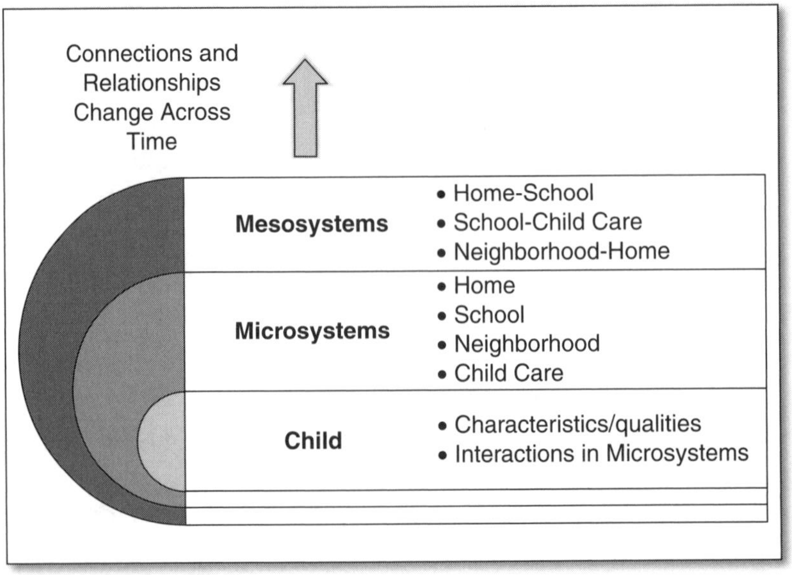

Rimm-Kaufman and Pianta (2000) proposed a more specific Ecological and Dynamic Model of Transition, for example, to explain how children's participation in a dynamic network of relationships (within home, school, peer, neighborhood, and other settings) influences their transition to school both directly and indirectly. The authors argued that these relationships predict subsequent relationships and either support or challenge children's adjustment and learning in school. Their adapted model emphasizes how relationships among these contexts change over time; this view is represented in Figure 1.1 by the arrow. From this view, Charlotte's relationships with her students and their parents and previous teachers create the potential for meaningful interactions to foster children's development. Recommended practices and school reform efforts based on these models, such as Comer's School Development Program (SDP), are mentioned in the following chapters.

Next, we briefly describe some of the major changes within the developing child from 4 to 8 years and then describe some changes in school contexts for children within this age range.

The Developmental Shift
From Early to Middle Childhood

Children's thinking, behavior, and relationships change dramatically from 4 to 8 years of age, particularly between 5 and 7. These changes are partly due to biological changes within children around this time period, such as reorganization of the frontal lobes, which has implications for many aspects of psychological and behavioral functioning. In addition, monumental changes occur in the important contexts of their lives at home and school, the authority figures, the number and kind of peers and friends, the activities, and the rules. In other words, "almost everything changes"

... 7-year-olds emerge as "different" from 5-year-olds as a result of the dynamic interplay between their developing abilities to make sense of their thoughts, feelings, and changing worlds, and the ways in which these worlds stimulate and respond to them.

(Haith & Sameroff, 1996, p. 437). Consistent with the ecological perspective, researchers explain that 7-year-olds emerge as "different" from 5-year-olds as a result of the dynamic interplay between their developing abilities to make sense of their thoughts, feelings, and changing worlds, and the ways in which these worlds stimulate and respond to them. Teachers who are aware of these dynamics are in a better position to understand and respond to children in the early years of school. This section focuses on a few important developmental changes occurring in children from 4 to 8 years and their school worlds. (A more complete list will be detailed in Table 1.1, p. 22.) These changes together promote the shift from early to middle childhood toward reason and responsibility, simply referred to as the "**5 to 7 developmental shift.**"

Changes in the Child

Major changes in children during the 5 to 7 shift include advances in (1) self-regulation abilities, (2) memory capacities and strategies, (3) self-reflective skills, (4) reasoning and logical thinking, and (5) perspective-taking. Each of these related abilities is discussed in turn.

Self-Regulation

Researchers suggest that many of the behavioral changes we see in children around this period of life are partly due to maturation of the brain, particularly the reorganization of the frontal lobes (e.g., Blair et al., 2007; Janowsky & Carper, 1996). These changes rouse memory, attentional, and self-reflection processes or "executive functioning" skills, which in turn enhance a number of other abilities, in particular, self-regulation (e.g., Blair, 2002). Teachers and researchers agree that **self-regulation skills** are critical for children's school readiness and later achievement. Self-regulation refers to children's ability to manage their emotions, focus their attention, and inhibit some behaviors while engaging in goal-directed behavior. Teachers often ask children to follow a series of steps in sequence that involve self-regulation. For example, teachers routinely direct children to do things, such as "put your reading books away, get your things ready for PE, and line up at the door." Self-regulation is involved as children inhibit their dominant response (keep reading) and substitute another response (get ready), demonstrating control of thought and action. Teachers also direct children to do things that involve emotional control as well as attentional, cognitive, and behavioral control. Children may need to control feelings of anger, frustration, and enthusiasm, for example, when they wait to raise their hand to respond to the teacher, take turns to participate in favorite activities, and stop engaging in desired activities when it is another child's turn. Suggestions for identifying and promoting children's self-regulation skills are included in Chapter 2.

Memory Capacities and Strategies

Children make important advances in memory capacities and use of strategies for encoding and retrieving new information between 5 and 9 years of age. (They have already developed remarkable memories for familiar activities and topics of great interest to them.) Children's short-term or working memory may expand, allowing them more "slots" for bits of information; for example, children typically recall four items (numbers or letters) at age 5 and six items at age 9 (e.g., Schneider & Pressley, 1997). Children's speed in processing information also increases substantially during this period; thus older children recognize and name objects more quickly than younger children (e.g., Kail, 2000). Their developing abilities to focus attention and reduce interference from irrelevant information (part of self-regulation) contribute to these abilities to remember new information (e.g., Pressley & McCormick, 2007). It is important for teachers to be aware of children's developing memory capacities during the early years of school; the amount of information children can process at one time may be limited (one to three "slots" fewer than adults). Teachers often support children by breaking down tasks into parts that are less demanding, such as providing a few directions or details at a time (e.g., put your jackets away, go to your desks, get out your books, move to your reading groups) until children have had time to "chunk" this related information or create a familiar script about the transition from recess to reading time.

Children's thinking and learning is also advanced by their emerging use of deliberate and effective **memory strategies** during these years. A strategy is defined as a conscious plan of action designed to achieve a goal perceived as under one's control (e.g., Pressley & McCormick, 2007). Preschoolers can use simple strategies to encode and recall things in familiar surroundings, such as looking at or naming a favorite toy that they want to play with later. They also demonstrate impressive abilities to recall information—about toys for example—when they elaborate or create stories about and interact with toys in pretend play. However, children before age 5 or 6 rarely use these strategies *intentionally* to encode information, and the strategies that they do use are often ineffective (Pressley & McCormick, 2007; Siegler & Alibali, 2005). This oversight may be partly because they do not recognize limitations in their memories; preschool and kindergarten children often predict that they can remember "everything" (all 20 items) when they are presented with recall tasks. Therefore, preschool and kindergarten teachers often need to provide cues for children to encode and retrieve information from memory. For example, teachers often help children find their "lost" belongings (an everyday event) by asking them about their previous activities (e.g., "Did you leave your jacket on the playground? Did you leave it in the lunchroom?"). They also frequently ask children to recall previous events in stories to aid their comprehension (e.g., "And then what happened?").

Children begin to use strategies to remember new information spontaneously around age 6. Simple rehearsal strategies are the first to develop (e.g., Siegler, 1998). For example, children might say the names of objects or digits to themselves over and over if they are told that they need to remember them. This is one example of how children's developing abilities to use language as a tool helps them regulate their thinking and behavior (e.g., Nelson, 1996; Vygotsky, 1978). Children this age also begin to use more sophisticated strategies, such as elaboration or organization strategies, *with cues and hints from adults* (e.g., Schneider & Bjorklund, 1998). For example, teachers can help children learn associations between words and their meanings through telling stories (elaboration) and categorizing information (organization), but they should not expect children to use these strategies on their own or monitor their effectiveness until the later school years (Pressley & McCormick, 2007). Interestingly, elementary children also begin to recognize their dependence on external aids to remember to do some things, and they commonly describe strategies such as "ask my mom to remind me" or "write a note."

Thus, children learn to better regulate their own thoughts as well as behaviors and emotions during this shift from early to middle childhood. Children become more strategic learners throughout the elementary and later school years, but they initiate these approaches to learning with sensitive guidance during the early years of school. Practical ideas for fostering self-regulated and strategic learning are included in later chapters.

Self-Reflection

Children's abilities to regulate their behaviors are enhanced by their emerging abilities for **self-reflection**. For example, the ability to ask oneself, "Am I doing this right?" "What else should I be doing?" creates opportunities for more adaptive functioning (e.g., Sameroff & Haith, 1996). Harter (1996, 2006) referred to the "I" self developing during this period, taking the

... implementing developmentally appropriate or learner-centered practices, such as those recommended throughout this book, should prevent or discourage children from adopting negative self-views as learners and maladaptive motivational patterns in the later elementary years.

"me" self as the object of evaluation. Advances in reflective abilities also create opportunities for children to better understand their own attributes and emotions. Children from 4 to 8 years typically shift from describing themselves in concrete or observable terms with a focus on physical characteristics (e.g., "I am tall, have brown hair . . .") or preferences and activities (e.g., "I like to build things") to describing qualities or trait generalizations based on behavior that are not immediately observable (e.g., "I am smart, honest . . ."). Children also begin to acknowledge that they can hold positive and negative attributes and feelings *at the same time* during this period. Thus, they often shift from describing themselves as "paragons of virtue" having mostly positive attributes to becoming more self-critical and describing both their positive and negative attributes (e.g., smart in reading, dumb in math; Harter, 1996). Scott depicts a child in transition (see *The Child's Window* at the end of this chapter). These shifts in self-understanding have enormous implications for children's motivation to learn in school. A theme is that children gradually develop the ability to make negative self-evaluations, which partly explains some of the typical declines in motivation observed at the end of primary grades (e.g., Dweck, 2002; Stipek, 2002). Children who believe they are less capable tend to shy away from challenging learning activities in some circumstances. Studies suggest that implementing developmentally appropriate or learner-centered practices, such as those recommended throughout this book, should prevent or discourage children from adopting negative self-views as learners and maladaptive motivational patterns in the later elementary years.

Reasoning and Logical Thinking

Children also make related advances in their reasoning and logical thinking during this period. Some researchers explain this change as a shift from "one- to two-sided" thinking (e.g., Cole, Cole, & Lightfoot, 2005). These characterizations of thinking derive partly from Piaget's well-known descriptions and explanations of the transformation from prelogical or preoperational thinking to logical or concrete-operational thinking in children from 5 to 7 years (e.g., Piaget, 1926, 1960). Reasoning in early childhood is characterized as one-sided (or egocentric) because children tend to focus or center on one perspective or one attribute or aspect of a problem or event at a time. During this period, children begin to consider two perspectives *simultaneously* or hold one attribute or aspect of a problem in mind while comparing it to another. We have seen how children's self-understanding reflects this cognitive shift. Children's abilities to reason about physical events can also be explained by their abilities to shift focus. For example, children come to understand that aspects of objects, such as size, length, density, and number, remain the same even though other aspects have changed. Piaget's famous conservation tasks reveal typical developments in children's thinking between 4 and 8 years (current research suggests that even very young children show budding conservation skills on simpler tasks). For example, 4-year-old children often claim that the amount of liquid increases or becomes "more" when it is poured into a taller glass. Presumably, children center on one quality, often its appearance. Children master conservation by around age 8, when they rely on their logic (e.g., "It's the same. It just looks different!") and can explain that the height of the glass is offset by its width (can coordinate and compare these changes). Other tasks are included in the *Practice Exercises* to reveal age-related changes in children's logic and reasoning.

Other significant changes related to advances in logical thinking or concrete operations are seen in children's abilities to classify and plan, both of which are important for school learning. Preschoolers are quite capable of classifying things; we are all probably familiar with young children's special collections of objects such as rocks, bugs, stuffed animals, and superhero toys. However, 4-year-old children tend not to organize their collections in hierarchies and according to multiple criteria like older children. Researchers explain that younger children have difficulty attending to superordinate classes (e.g., bugs) and included subclasses (e.g., grasshoppers) simultaneously; although there are notable exceptions to this rule when children spend a great deal of time learning about a subject (e.g., dinosaurs) and become "experts."

Children age 8 and older develop more sophisticated classification systems for their collections, such as organizing baseball cards according to players' teams, positions, and ranks. Children's learning about a range of academic subjects is influenced by their developing classification skills.

Children's abilities to plan their activities also depend to some extent on their abilities to decenter and attend to multiple aspects of a problem. To make a plan, children must keep in mind their present condition, their goal for the future, and what to do to get from the present to the future. Preschoolers vary widely in their abilities to plan ahead (Hyson, Copple, & Jones, 2006). Children's emerging planning skills are often revealed while they are engaged in play. Between 4 and 8 years of age, children often make partial plans in advance (step-by-step), but they continue to have difficulties making systematic plans toward goals without assistance (Siegler & Alibali, 2005). Early childhood educators are able to help children improve their planning skills in programs such as *Tools of the Mind* (Bodrova & Leong, 2007), which is introduced in Chapter 4.

Perspective-Taking

Cognitive advances such as perspective-taking have obvious implications for children's abilities to understand and interact effectively with others. For example, they gradually become better able to consider and practice the Golden Rule, which has positive implications for their social behavior. In addition, two-sided thinking relates to advances in children's abilities to compare their observable behavior and skills with others during this period. These comparisons sometimes influence their evaluations of self and others as well as their performance behavior. For example, children might begin to dwell on perceived inadequacies and expect less of self and/or others. Children also advance simple abilities to compare their own unobservable thoughts, desires, and beliefs with others, developing more sophisticated "theories of mind."

Children's developing **theories of mind** have been extensively studied in the past two decades, demonstrating that by

4 years of age, children have a good head start toward under-standing the minds of others. For example, they can recognize that others believe or know different things than they do, like where a toy is hidden. Thus, they are sometimes able to iden-tify false beliefs to make sense of unexpected behavior, such as their teacher's search for a book in the wrong place. They understand that their teacher believes it is somewhere else and that this belief is different from their own. Researchers propose that during the 5 to 7 shift, children advance from merely acknowledging that people have different beliefs about the "real world" (a copy view) to beginning to under-stand that people also fit the real world to their beliefs (an interpretive or constructivist view; Chandler & Lalonde, 1996). For example, in a clever experiment with Raggedy Ann and Andy puppets, Chandler and Lalonde (1996) found that 7-year-olds were more likely than 5-year-olds to report that Ann and Andy would disagree about an event because of their different dispositions and explain that the characters would not "think with the same brain." We cannot overstate the tremendous influence of these social cognitive advances for children's behavior and interactions in school and else-where. The implications for working with children in class-rooms are discussed in subsequent chapters.

Summary: Changes in the Child

In sum, from the modern scientific view, children *do* think, feel, and behave quite differently at age 7 or 8 than they did when they were 4 or 5. However, this does not mean that 5-year-olds cannot do some of the things that 7-year-olds do; they just don't typically do so. Current researchers explain this shift in different ways, but many point to the important role of children's developing abilities to reflect on their thoughts and experiences that coincide with neurological changes, as well as changes in their social worlds or ecologies. Changes in children's school worlds are highlighted next.

The contemporary view of the child implied in these descriptions of developmental change is consistent with constructivist or social-constructivist theoretical perspectives, as well as ecological approaches to understanding development. These perspectives emphasize the role of children as active participants in the physical and social worlds that propel their own development. Constructivist perspectives and classroom practices are described in Chapter 4.

Changes in School Contexts

Children from 4 to 8 years experience significant changes in their social environments, or ecological shifts, most prominently at home and school. Researchers argue that virtually everything about children's lives change when they move from primarily family contexts to school contexts, even for those with preschool experience (e.g., Kagan & Neville, 1996; Ladd, 1996; Rimm-Kaufman & Pianta, 2000). Consequently, children's roles, responsibilities, and relationships (the other three R's) change dramatically and impact their development.

> . . . virtually everything about children's lives change when they move from primarily family contexts to school contexts, even for those with preschool experience.

Typical changes from preschool to kindergarten to the primary grades involve increasing emphasis on academic skills, independence, and social interactions with a wide range of peers, often accompanied by a reduction in opportunities for families to provide a secure base for their children to face these enormous challenges. In other words, the goals, demands, and the nature of the classroom environment change, along with the ecology surrounding the new environments (Rimm-Kaufman & Pianta, 2000). Children are thrust into these new environments when they reach certain ages, not necessarily when they are "ready." Some children adjust well to their new environments, and some do not; the next chapter focuses on how school environments affect different children's adjustment, future relationships, and learning.

School and classroom environments typically change from preschool to elementary school in the ways listed in Table 1.1 (e.g., Ladd, 1996; Pianta, Cox, & Snow, 2007). Children move from smaller settings with higher adult-child ratios to larger settings with lower adult-child ratios. Children often travel in different ways to these settings (e.g., walk, ride school buses) and have to find familiar people in larger playgrounds and their classrooms in larger buildings. They also participate in increasingly "formal" schooling activities, spending more time working on structured academic tasks and less time in semistructured activities such as play as they move across grade levels. In addition, many new external rules and regulations are introduced to manage their behavior and time.

Children also spend more time with peers and less time with adults. Opportunities for interacting with peers of different ages decrease as they move from preschool to age-segregated elementary classrooms. In addition, they receive more critical feedback about their skills and behavior and are increasingly compared with their classmates and evaluated according to performance standards. Thus, children are gradually more pressed to "achieve among equals" (Ladd, 1996) across the primary grades.

Relationships with teachers also change as children compete with more classmates for their time and attention. In addition, relationships with peers change as composition of peer networks change from grade to grade (especially from preschool to kindergarten). Thus, children often need to figure out how to join new groups and make new friends with unfamiliar children from backgrounds very different from their own.

Furthermore, children's parents become less involved in their school activities as they progress through higher grade levels. Although parental involvement is relatively high in the early school years, it typically drops off between preschool and kindergarten and gradually declines thereafter if schools have not made efforts to encourage involvement a priority. Thus, teachers need to be especially cognizant of the critical role they play as *the* adult providers of security for young children during the many hours they spend at school. This role is discussed in Chapter 3.

Table 1.1 summarizes some typical developmental shifts in contexts and children.

Table 1.1   The Developmental Shift From Early to Middle Childhood (4–8 years)

Biological/Physical	• Reorganization of the frontal lobes • Refinement of fine and gross motor skills
Cognitive/Social/ Emotional/Behavioral	• Increase in memory capacity and strategic remembering • Increase in control of attention, behavior, and emotions (self-regulation) • Increase in self-reflection • Increase in logical and two-sided thinking; classification • Decrease in egocentrism; improved perspective-taking • Enhanced "theory of mind"
Social Contexts (in general)	• Increased participation in peer groups • Deliberate instruction in many areas • Play without direct adult supervision • Golden Rule morality • Increase in social comparison • Increase in expectations for independent and responsible behavior • Changes in relations with caretakers
School and Classroom Contexts (in particular)	• Lower adult-child ratios • More time with same-age, unfamiliar peers; changes in peer networks • Larger physical environments to navigate • New classroom and playground rules and regulations • Increase in critical feedback about skills and behavior based on standards and comparisons with classmates • Changes in relations with teachers

Researchers, educators, and policymakers recognize that these dramatic changes in school contexts present tremendous challenges for children in a phase of life fraught with potential. Children can be guided toward positive routes through school, or alternatively, onto negative ones. Thus, a great deal of current attention is given to promoting high quality relationships and instructional practices in classrooms based on contemporary perspectives and aligning practices across preschool and the early grades of school to create smooth transitions for children (e.g., Bogard & Takanishi, 2005; Pianta et al., 2007). The following view depicts a child who has adjusted well to first grade but continues to need a great deal of support for his developing competencies. Scott's description also illustrates typical ways of thinking and behaving of children in the midst of the 5 to 7 shift.

The Child's Window

Scott is 6 years old. He describes himself as "a boy with brown hair. I have a dog and a bike and a new videogame at home. I like to play soccer, but sometimes I get hurt...." He has been in first grade for "a long time." He likes his teacher because "she is nice and teaches me stuff." He likes sharing what he's learned in reading with his parents at home because "they like to listen." His favorite activities in school are reading, recess, and "following the snail trails on the sidewalk." He still misses kindergarten where he was able to "ride bikes and build things."

When asked to rate his competencies, he indicates that he is very smart ("my mom says"), pretty good at reading ("I can't read all the words and the long books"), very good at math ("I just know!"), and good at art. When asked if he had friends at school, he said "yes" and described yesterday's activities with two boys. In response to, "What do your friends James and Enrique think of you?" he exclaimed, "I don't know what they think about!"

Scott was attentive throughout this 20-minute "interview"; he occasionally moved off-topic and became fidgety toward the end of the session. Earlier assessments of his behavioral regulation indicated that he was on course with his peers, and his teacher described his attentional skills as typical for a boy his age. His teacher rated his early academic competencies as "average." She is working with him on reading comprehension; she wants

> *to see him ask more questions and make more connections to what they read in class together. She describes him as "a little immature" and nonassertive, especially in groups. In general, she reports that he is "well adjusted" to school and eagerly participates in most class activities. She has no serious concerns.*

TEACHERS' PERSPECTIVES ON DEVELOPMENT AND PRACTICE

Teachers' understandings of child development are important because their beliefs influence their intentions and plans for educational practices, their actual interactions with children, and in turn, their students' adjustment and learning in school. Unfortunately, studies show that not all educators embrace contemporary views of children's development based on dynamic models and current research outlined in this book. Instead, many harbor views of children's development based on more traditional perspectives, such as simple behavioral or bio-maturational views of development, focusing on *either* how the teacher impacts children's learning and behavior through reinforcement (behavioral) *or* how children's already developed competencies affect or limit their learning and behavior (bio-maturational). (See Table 1.2, pp. 26–27, for sample descriptions of contemporary and traditional views.) Some studies suggest that teachers with contemporary views are more likely to endorse and consistently implement practices that foster children's development and learning than teachers with traditional or mixed views (e.g., Daniels & Shumow, 2003; McCombs & Whisler, 1997; Stipek & Byler, 1997; Wang, Elicker, McMullen, & Mao, 2008).

Educational and developmental psychologists have derived principles and practices stemming from current theoretical perspectives and research on child development and learning that have guided studies on teacher beliefs. Two efforts made by major professional organizations to bridge the gap between current knowledge and classroom practice are noteworthy. An earlier American Psychological Association taskforce (APA, 1997) produced **"learner-centered"** principles from psychological research that have inspired professional development practices and research (e.g., McCombs & Whisler, 1997). The National Association for the Education of Young Children periodically updates **"developmentally appropriate"** belief statements and sample practices to guide programs for children from birth to age 8 (Copple & Bredekamp, 2009). (See Resources) The beliefs and practices endorsed by these organizations are similar to those referred to as "child centered" or "student centered." Table 1.2 provides a few sample descriptions of developmentally appropriate or learner-centered beliefs consistent with contemporary theoretical perspectives and research and some sample descriptions of developmentally inappropriate or non-learner-centered beliefs aligned with more traditional beliefs. These descriptions or items are adapted from several measures used in research on preschool and primary-grade teacher beliefs (e.g., McCombs, Daniels, & Perry, 2008; Smith, 1993; Stipek & Byler, 1997). Classroom practices based on contemporary developmental perspectives are described in the following chapters.

CHAPTER SUMMARY

The *Window* into Charlotte's classroom at the beginning of the chapter provided us with a brief view of a teacher who practiced what she preached and believed. Her intentions to implement practices considered developmentally appropriate were based on her studies of contemporary theories and research on children's development and learning in graduate school; her program of study also emphasized learning about children's home cultures and languages. She struggled and made some mistakes her first year as all teachers do, but she developed caring, respectful relationships with her students and (most of) their families to create a positive classroom climate. By midyear, her classroom appeared to be managed almost entirely by her first graders. Thus, she could devote most of her time to intentional instruction, and her students learned to read in two

Table 1.2 Contemporary and Traditional Teacher Beliefs About Children's Development and Learning: Sample Descriptions

Contemporary Beliefs	Traditional Beliefs
• Addressing children's social, emotional, and physical needs is just as important to learning as meeting their intellectual needs.	• The most important job as a teacher is to help students meet well-established standards; basic academic skills should be the teacher's top priority. Children should be retained if they have not mastered basic skills at grade level.
• One of the best ways children learn is through active exploration in an environment prepared by teachers.	• Children learn best through repetition and practice.
• Children's enthusiasm for a task is more important than how well they do.	• Teachers should emphasize quality in final products.
• Seeing things from children's perspectives is key to their learning and good performance in school.	• Giving rewards and extra privileges for good performance is one of the best ways to motivate children to learn.
• Creating caring relationships with children is critical for their learning.	
• To maximize learning, teachers need to help children reflect on and discuss their thoughts and feelings.	• During a lesson, children should not be able to interrupt a teacher to relate personal experiences.

• Subject areas should be related to each other and children's real experiences and participation in concrete activities.	• Instruction should be clearly divided into separate subject areas.
• Children are able to participate in setting classroom rules.	• One of the most important things to teach children is how to follow rules and to do what is expected of them in the classroom.
• Children should be able to choose alternative ways of approaching planned activities.	
• Curriculum should respond primarily to individual differences in ability and interest.	• Curriculum should respond primarily to grade-level expectations.
• Opportunities for interacting with peers and teachers in small groups should predominate over whole group and individual experience.	• For most of the time, children should be expected to work quietly on their own and in teacher-led small reading groups.
• Teacher observation and informal assessments are the most valid way to gauge children's learning and performance.	• Tests are the most valid way to assess children's performance.
• Teachers should deal with parents mainly informally, encouraging them to participate in the classroom and at home.	• Teachers should deal with parents mainly through formally scheduled meetings and conferences.

languages! Just as important for her students' future development was the fact that many of their parents learned to be more
comfortable and involved at school. Rationales and suggestions
for creating developmentally appropriate (or learner-centered)
relationships and classroom practices like these are presented
in the remaining chapters of this book.

Questions to Ponder

1. Think about yourself as the child in the middle of the
ecological model in Figure 1.1. How would you explain
your own adjustment to school in the early grades (if
you can recall) or later grades in terms of your skills
and dispositions and multiple contextual influences
(e.g., home, school, neighborhood)? How did experiences in these contexts influence you?

2. What are your beliefs about child development? Do
you support more of the contemporary or traditional
belief statements in Table 1.2 or some combination?
Why? How do your beliefs relate to how you might
implement activities in the classroom?

(Note that these questions are intended to promote self-
reflection, not provide a valid assessment of beliefs.)

Practice Exercises

1. **Interviews.** Invite children ages 4 or 5 and ages 7 or
8 years to participate in an "interview" with you. Tell
them this will help you learn more about how they think
and feel. Ask a series of questions to reveal their understandings of self and others; samples are provided here.
Compare responses of older and younger children. Do
their responses reflect typical developmental changes
noted in this chapter? (Note: Do not be concerned if the
younger children reveal very little in words.)

   a. Tell me about yourself. What are you like? What
   kind of person are you? What are you not like?

Sample probes: Can you tell me something about the way that you look? Feel? Think? What are you good at? Not so good at? What would your mom or dad say about you? What would your friends say? What would your teacher say? Do you agree with what _____ might say?

b. Tell me about one of your friends. What is his/her name? What is he/she like? Sample probes: How is he/she different from you? The same as you? Can you tell me something about how he/she looks/feels/thinks different from you?

2. **Piagetian-Like Conservation Tasks.** Invite individual children ages 4 or 5 and ages 7 or 8 years to participate in a brief activity with you. To examine the child's understanding of conservation of mass, show two equal balls of playdough or clay and ask, "Do both balls have just as much clay/dough?" When the child agrees that they are the same, then roll one of the balls into a hot dog shape as he observes. Then ask, "Now do the balls have the same amount of dough or are they different? Why did you say that they were the same/different?" To examine the child's understanding of conservation of number, show two lines with the same number (5–7) of small objects, such as candies or pennies, equal in length. Ask if the lines are the same. When the child agrees that they are the same (some will move the objects a bit to line up), spread out one line in front of the child so that it looks longer than the other one. Then ask, "Now do the lines have the same number of candies/pennies or are they different? Why?" Compare older and younger children's responses and check to see if they correspond to typical changes in children's thinking described in this chapter.

3. **Games**. Invite children of different ages to play a familiar board game with you. Before you begin, ask them to explain the rules to you (tell them you don't remember). Their explanations are likely to reveal something

about their abilities to take your perspective, think about several things simultaneously, and plan ahead. Then play the game, periodically asking questions about their strategies and observing their abilities to attend and regulate their behavior. Again, compare older and younger children's behaviors and consider whether they reflect typical developmental shifts.

Key Words

Ecological perspective

5 to 7 developmental shift

Self-regulation

Memory strategies

Self-reflection

Theories of mind

Learner-centered principles and practices

Developmentally appropriate practices (DAP)

2

Early School Adjustment

Fostering Children's Adjustment and Self-Regulation

Window Into Practice

Trudy is a kindergarten teacher in a suburban-rural area. She has been teaching for over 20 years, mostly in the primary grades. She is grateful for her small class size this year—only 18 children—because she felt she could get to know each child. This group was fairly diverse; children were from a variety of backgrounds, mostly White, Latino/a, and Asian from low- to middle-income families, although there were some from high-income families. Trudy looked and behaved like one might expect of a kindergarten teacher; she demonstrated warm, nurturing behavior toward the children in her classroom by frequently bending down to talk eye-to-eye with them individually, putting a hand on their backs. Her enthusiasm for teaching was especially evident when she read stories to children on the rug. She was quite dramatic, using different voices for characters and exaggerated expressions, and she involved the children by asking them to think about the characters' feelings and predict what would happen next. ALL of the children were engaged during story time.

Trudy's classroom was fairly large and she maintained a high quality setting, according to National Association for the Education of Young Children standards and early childhood education researchers. Many separate learning centers were available with a variety of materials for reading, writing, math, dramatic play, art, and science (some). The reading area included a listening center and several books depicting people from different backgrounds and places. These centers surrounded small group arrangements of desks and chairs for children. In addition, it was a cheerful classroom. There was a large, colorful rug for whole group meeting and reading times, several fuzzy animals in cages, a few cozy seats for reading and relaxing, cubbies for individual children's belongings, and interesting art and work by children displayed throughout the classroom. The teacher's desk was set to the side, rarely used while the children were there.

Trudy's friendly nature and classroom environment fostered expected responses from children. A month after school began, most children appeared comfortable and familiar with the routine. These observations were supported by "interviews" with selected children about their experiences. Most of the children reported that they liked school either pretty or very much, and almost all reported that their teacher liked and cared about them very much. Children's reasons for liking school were predictably idiosyncratic, ranging from "I like to ride the bus" or "I like playing on the monkey bars" to "I'm learning how to read." A few reported concerns such as "I don't like waiting for my Grandma to pick me up for lunch" and "I don't know. I just don't like it." One child had a particularly difficult time expressing his feelings but eventually reported that he liked to do "other things better." This child came from an exceptionally high quality preschool/child care program.

Classroom observers and the teacher were not surprised to find that favorable feelings about school were not unanimous. Observers noted that although there were numerous appropriate classroom materials available, children did not spend much time in the learning centers on a daily basis. Trudy expressed considerable frustration with current pressures to "get children to read so early" and had adjusted her schedule this year to spend more time with reading groups because she had several children with no preschool experience and few literacy activities at home. She found out about children's backgrounds through her participation in orientation meetings with parents and a new school readiness program—Kindercamp— where she taught a simulated kindergarten program for a few weeks during the summer that was geared for children from low-income families. She was determined, however, to free up more time soon for children to play in all the learning centers and "be kindergarteners."

Trudy's and her students' experiences in kindergarten are not unusual today. They reflect concerns with "school readiness" and notions that small class sizes are ideal for fostering young children's adjustment and learning. They reflect some notions of "best practice" currently advocated by developmental and educational researchers and professional organizations. Their experiences also reflect conflicts about the relative academic versus social nature of kindergarten and the role of play in school, inspired by the No Child Left Behind Act's press toward meeting performance standards. Trudy is an example of an experienced teacher who is coping with these concerns and conflicts quite well and is continuing to implement practices considered developmentally appropriate by experts in the field. Students in her elementary school are also coping and meeting state standards (however, her school has not received awards for excellence like some other schools in the area).

This chapter focuses on "readiness" of *children for school* and *school for children* in the early years. We look at research showing how qualities of children and schools influence children's early and later adjustment and achievement. We explain how some qualities associated with positive adjustment, such as children's self-regulation behaviors, can be fostered. We also relay recommendations made for transitional activities to foster early school adjustment. (Recommendations for enhancing relationships and classroom practices are described more fully in subsequent chapters.) In addition, we identify some common problems with children associated with difficult adjustments and how educators can offset these difficulties. Finally, we examine children's perspectives and their importance during the early school years.

EARLY SCHOOL ADJUSTMENT MODELS

As we saw in Chapter 1, changes in environments and expectations present challenges for children in the early school years. Children's success in dealing with these changes is influenced by their own qualities and supports available, as well as other factors such as the quality of school practices. Developmental and educational psychologists are concerned about identifying signs of and ways to promote early school adjustment partly because of their future impact on children's development and well-being throughout the school years. The models used to explain children's early school adjustment are consistent with dynamic ecological models of development. A central assumption of these person-by-environment models is that the origins of early school adjustment (i.e., responses to task demands) lie in both the child and in the child's interpersonal environment (e.g., Ladd, 1996; Rimm-Kaufman & Pianta, 2000). Figure 2.1 depicts a simple model illustrating child × environment interactions across the early grades in school. Trudy created a supportive context for children with various skills and dispositions to cope with new school demands. Her intention to provide more stimulating learning activities will likely enhance children's positive feelings about school.

School readiness has been generally conceived of as the skills and knowledge that children bring to school associated

Figure 2.1   Child × Environment Model of Early School
                  Adjustment

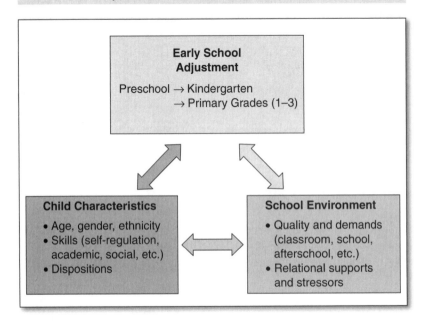

with later adjustment and achievement, despite the limited success of child readiness measures to predict later outcomes (Pianta & Cox, 2002; Snow, 2007). Today we emphasize how schools prepare for children. We attend to child characteristics first and then to classroom characteristics and relationships that help to better explain children's school adjustment. **School adjustment** is reflected in children's attitudes and emotional experiences in school, their involvement or engagement with the school environment, as well as their performance in school (Birch & Ladd, 1997; Ladd, 1996).

READINESS OF THE CHILD

In this section, we discuss child qualities commonly associated with school readiness. We begin with factors such as age, sex, and preschool experience, and then attend to three major domains of readiness related to the development of self-regulation skills (control of thoughts, emotions, and motivated learning behavior).

Age, Sex, and Preschool Experience

The most controversial questions concerning children's readiness for school are probably, "Do older children do better?" and "Is preschool necessary?" Educators, parents, and policymakers have debated the question about whether age matters for many years, recognizing discrepancies between states and countries in age requirements for entry into school. In the United States, although not currently mandated, most children begin school in kindergarten at around age 5. However, for a number of reasons (including postponing school entry or "redshirting" to allow for further growth), age spans in kindergarten classrooms may vary from 1 to 2 years (Vecchiotti, 2003). Today, researchers usually recommend against delaying an eligible child's entry into kindergarten. From a review of studies on entrance age, Stipek (2002a) argued that educational experiences in school contribute more to children's adjustment and cognitive competencies than age or maturation. Although older children may initially perform better academically, these positive effects are slight and tend to fade across the early grades of school.

Parents may be particularly concerned with sending young boys to school "too early" because of their relative immaturity. Recent research supports these reservations to some extent: Kindergarten teachers have reported that boys show less effective self-regulatory skills and engagement in learning in the classroom than girls (e.g., Rimm-Kaufman, Curby, Grimm, Nathanson, & Brock, 2009; Xue & Meisels, 2004). However, it is important to note that such sex differences are not found in all studies. Although boys may be at greater risk for problems in school for several reasons (e.g., Ladd, 1996; Raver, Garner, & Smith-Donald, 2007), researchers do not recommend delaying their entry into school. Today, parents may also be reluctant to send their eligible (age-ready) children to kindergarten without preschool because of extensive media campaigns promoting its importance. Again, parents' concerns may be partly justified: Research shows that children, especially those from disadvantaged backgrounds (e.g., poverty), benefit from quality preschool programs (e.g., Pianta, Cox, & Snow, 2007; Zigler, Gilliam, & Jones, 2006). However, researchers do not recommend delaying entry of eligible children to kindergarten if they have not attended preschool. Stipek (2002a) urged that we focus instead on making school ready for children and tailoring practices to their diverse skills and experiences, rather than making children ready for school. This case is echoed by many other developmental scientists and early childhood experts.

...we [should] focus instead on making school ready for children and tailoring practices to their diverse skills and experiences, rather than making children ready for school.

Domains of Readiness

What skills and dispositions of children tend to foster their adjustment and later achievement? Kindergarten teachers often focus on social and emotional rather than preacademic aspects of school readiness (e.g., Dockett & Perry, 2004). However,

some recent studies indicate that teachers increasingly emphasize preacademic skills, especially for children from low-
income families (e.g., Snow, 2007). Researchers have studied a
long "laundry list" of intellectual, social, emotional, behavioral,
and (pre)academic skills related to adjustment, and they have
recently examined relationships between key *domains of readiness* skills. Snow (2007), for example, proposed that two
domains of child competence are especially important because
they mediate or indirectly affect many aspects of children's
learning and development: their "executive functioning" (e.g.,
attentional skills) and their "approaches to learning." A third
domain includes children's abilities to regulate their emotions
as mediators of academic readiness and school adjustment
(Raver et al., 2007). These three **domains of readiness** related to
self-regulation are discussed in turn: (a) executive function
(control of cognitive processes), (b) emotional regulation (control of emotional processes), and (c) approaches to learning
(control of motivated behavior). Although a few researchers
distinguish between self-*regulation* as pursuit of one's own
goals and self-*control* as pursuit of goals imposed by others, we
use these terms interchangeably here because many goals that
children pursue in real classroom life are "in between" goals
that are truly valued by self and others (Boekaerts, 2006). Later
we look at how to foster children's self-regulation skills.

Blair (2002) has advanced a developmental (neuroscience)
model of school readiness that highlights the role of self-
regulation, regulation of attention and selective strategy use
in executing cognitive tasks, and regulation of emotions
in appropriate social responding. He argued that children's
self-regulatory skills underlie many of the behaviors and
attributes associated with school adjustment. Furthermore, he
suggested that self-regulation skills may be just as key for predicting school success as intelligence.

Control of Cognitive Processes (Executive Function)

Blair and his colleagues focused on studies of the cognitive
aspects of self-regulation that go under the general heading of
executive function (EF; Blair et al., 2007), the first domain of

readiness. Based on their review, they defined EF as "cognitive or supervisory processes associated with the active maintenance of information in working memory, the appropriate shifting and sustaining of attention among goal-relevant aspects of a given task or problem, and the inhibition of prepotent or extraneous information and responding within a given task context" (p. 151). In other words, EF involves efficiently managing one's thought processes. These processes are sometimes referred to as cognitive **effortful control (EC)** processes. Children high in EF or EC intentionally control their attention and behavior as needed. As discussed in Chapter 1, children develop more sophisticated control skills during the shift from early to middle childhood. Simpler abilities developed during the preschool years impact children's academic readiness. For example, Blair and his colleagues (2007) found that preschoolers in Head Start programs who could control their tapping behavior on an experimental task had higher math and literacy skills when they were in kindergarten. In a similar study, preschool children who were better able to sustain their attention and inhibit their impulses on a task ("heads-to-toes" game) had higher emergent literacy and math skills later on in the year (McClelland et al., 2007). (See the *Practice Exercises* for ways to reveal children's aspects of EF skills using similar tasks.)

Preschoolers' attentional and inhibitory skills also predict their social and language skills, as well as their academic skills in kindergarten (NICHD ECCRN, 2003).

A recent study indicates that children high in EC skills have better social relationships and participate more in class activities, which in turn predicts their greater academic performance (Valiente, Lemery-Chalfant, Swanson, & Reiser, 2008). These researchers stated simply, ". . . EC provides students with relational and motivational advantages that help them perform well" (p. 74). Thus, research supports the argument that children's developing abilities to regulate their thoughts and behaviors (EF or EC) indirectly influence many aspects of school readiness and adjustment.

Researchers also investigate how adults influence children's EC and other self-regulation skills. For example, a recent study showed that mothers' effective use of limit set-ting (i.e., clarity, consistency, and follow through with direc-tives when required) and scaffolding (i.e., intervention only when needed) during play predicted their preschool children's EC (Lengua, Honorado, & Bush, 2006). These researchers point out that children in high-risk settings (e.g., poverty) are potentially in jeopardy for lower EC skills and adjustment difficulties due to lower quality parenting skills. Fortunately, studies show that interventions can improve aspects of EC and behavioral regulation. For example, impul-sive children can be taught to talk to themselves as a means of controlling their behavior (Reid, Trout, & Schartz, 2005). Blair et al. (2007) also reported that children in training studies—involving game-like practice on computer-based tasks—show improvements in some EF skills, as well as increases in neural activity related to these skills and behavior. Classroom-based "interventions" or practices are introduced later.

Blair et al. (2007) proposed that the neuroscience model for school readiness focused on self-regulation is highly consistent with child-centered or contemporary (developmentally appro-priate) educational approaches advocated here. "A central tenet of the child-centered, progressive approach to education is that knowledge acquisition occurs more effectively when children are engaged and using the cognitive abilities that characterize EF" (p. 157). They argued that these contempo-rary approaches intentionally foster improvements in EF and related critical thinking skills to promote engagement in school learning more than traditional or "back to basics" approaches.

Control of Emotional Processes (Emotional Regulation)

The second major domain of skills expected to mediate school readiness and adjustment involves **emotional regula-tion (ER)** skills. ER is related to but distinct from the more cognitively focused EF self-regulation skills (Hyson et al., 2006). Children with high ER skills can manage the intensity of emotional responses—such as anger, fear, pleasure, sadness—to be appropriate for the situation. For example, children may need to manage feelings of fear when they enter new classrooms so that they attend to their teacher's directions and join appropriate activities. Children who have difficulties regulating fearful reactions might cling to parents or teachers (if they can) or stand to the side of the class, unable to figure out how to become involved. Fortunately, as we will see, teachers are able to help these children manage their emotions and inhibitions. Effective ER guides cognitive and social interactions and enhances rather than jeopardizes well-being.

According to Hyson and colleagues (2006), children acquiring ER skills are increasingly able to do the following:

- Keep in touch with their own emotional responses.
- Stop themselves from displaying inappropriate behavior motivated by strong positive or negative feelings.
- Calm, distract, or soothe themselves when strong feelings threaten to overwhelm them.
- Use varied and flexible coping strategies to change the intensity of their emotions.
- Coordinate feelings, thought, and actions to reach goals that are important to them.
- Use emotions to help focus and sustain attention.
- Influence others by the use of emotions.
- Follow the standards of their culture about when and how to show emotions (p. 23).

Children with serious regulatory difficulties are on pathways that tend to alienate them from teachers and their classmates and from access to learning opportunities.

Research suggests that children come to school with relatively stable ER abilities (e.g., Raver et al., 2007). Problems with ER, particularly with the regulation of negative emotions (e.g., venting anger), predict both social and academic difficulties in the later years of school. Children with serious regulatory difficulties are on pathways that tend to alienate them from teachers and their classmates and from access to learning opportunities. Thus, helping children tame their emotions has become a priority of early education programs, such as *High Scope* and *Tools for Thinking* (see Resources). Suggestions for working with children prone to difficulties with anger and aggressive behavior, as well as anxiety and inhibited behavior, are presented later.

Teachers can support ER by talking about emotions in the context of everyday activities or stories. Providing children with language labels for their emotional experiences is expected to help them internalize and use these to express and regulate their own responses. In addition, teachers can model appropriate expressions and behavioral responses, as well as provide constructive guidance for children to manage their emotions in everyday activities. Of course, such assistance must be provided in the context of positive relationships with children (see Chapter 3). Vivian Paley, a well-known early educator and author of many books, demonstrates brilliant ways of communicating with children about their feelings during play and literacy activities. For example, in one of her classic works, *White Teacher*, she describes how she helps a boy identify and eventually curtail his angry, aggressive outbursts during play. Specific recommendations by educators and researchers for promoting ER and EC skills are included in Table 2.2; further information is provided in Resources.

Control of Motivated Behavior (Approaches To Learning)

The third major domain, **approaches to learning,** captures a broad range of skills or dispositions of children linked to ER (emotional regulation) and EC (effortful control) that influences their learning, early adjustment, and later achievement in school (Snow, 2007). For example, school-related attitudes, persistence, and work-related skills fall into this category. Work-related skills include paying attention to the teacher, participating in groups, and engaging in classroom tasks. Behavioral indicators of children's positive approaches to learning in the early grades of school are shown in Table 2.1; researchers have included markers such as these on teacher surveys (e.g., Betts & Rotenberg,

Table 2.1   Children's Positive Approaches to Learning in the Classroom: Sample Behavioral Indicators

Orientation/Attitudes Toward School

- Laughs or smiles easily
- Approaches the teacher comfortably
- Approaches new activities with enthusiasm
- Is curious and eager to learn
- Is optimistic and recovers from setbacks quickly (sees the glass "half full")

On-Task Involvement/Engagement in Class Activities

- Listens carefully to teacher's instructions
- Responds promptly to teacher's requests
- Uses classroom materials responsibly
- Shows interest in activities
- Returns to selected activities after interruptions
- Sticks to the task at hand, even during longer or unpleasant tasks
- Participates in group activities

Other Work Habits

- Seeks challenges
- Persists in the face of difficulties
- Asks for help when needed
- Follows classroom procedures
- Works well independently
- Makes plans to reach goals
- Anticipates consequences of behaviors
- Works toward goals
- Uses time wisely

Social Behavior (Regulation)

- Waits turn to talk in class when appropriate
- Does not disrupt others
- Does not get into fights

2007; Rimm-Kaufman et al., 2009) and other descriptions of school readiness and adjustment. Findings from a recent longitudinal study suggest that preschoolers do indeed "bring" some of these approaches with them to kindergarten, at least for the first few months of school (Daniels, 2009). Such approaches are associated with early academic success and can be encouraged by adopting the classroom practices that are described later.

Associations With Later School Achievement

In sum, children's abilities to regulate their cognitive, emotional, and motivational behavior in the classroom during the early years contribute to their success in social and academic domains of school functioning. Researchers argue that these skills provide the mechanism for children to access instructional resources in educational settings for optimal learning and development (e.g., Konold & Pianta, 2005; Kress & Elias, 2006). These skills are reflected in important areas of social functioning that teachers and researchers deem critical for early school adjustment: (a) positive conduct (nondisruptive or nonexternalizing behavior); (b) prosocial, cooperative behavior; and (c) positive relationships (and lack of conflict) with teachers. They are also reflected in academic functioning. For example, Blair et al. (2007) proposed that children's developing EF skills are reflected in (and fostered by) their abilities to conduct common mathematical activities in the early elementary grades (i.e., pattern completion exercises). In a recent examination of major long-term studies, Duncan and a number of prominent researchers (2007) found that early attention skills are indeed predictive of later academic achievement.

Other Skills and Combinations: Profiles of School Readiness

Duncan and his colleagues (2007) also looked at how a number of children's academic and social skills assessed at school entry influenced their later achievement. They found that early math skills (i.e., knowledge of numbers, ordinality) were the most powerful predictors of later academic performance. Children's early language and literacy skills (i.e., vocabulary; knowing letters, words, beginning and ending word sounds) were also predictive. Contrary to expectations, they did not find evidence for the long-term influence of social skills demonstrated by children *at school entry.* They suggested that social skills emerging *during* the early elementary years may be more critical for academic learning (refer to Chapter 1). Other developmental researchers agree. On the other hand, children with positive social skills *and* other readiness skills do appear to have an initial head start, as we shall see.

Developmental researchers have recently identified subgroups of children that display similar patterns of strengths and weaknesses in different domains of competence. For example, Konold and Pianta (2005) derived the following **profiles of school readiness** likely to be found among typically developing preschool children on the basis of cognitive (EF) and social skills:

- *High cognitive and mild externalizing (22%).* This group scored highest on cognitive measures and had slightly above average externalizing behaviors (e.g., aggression). This group outperformed all others on achievement measures in first grade.
- *High social competence (24%).* This group had the highest social skills and the lowest externalizing behaviors and average cognitive skills. This group performed better than most groups on several achievement measures in first grade.
- *Low to average social and cognitive skills (20%).* This group had somewhat lower social skills and low to average cognitive skills.
- *Social and externalizing problems (17%).* This group had moderately low social skills and high externalizing behavior, average cognitive skills, and some attention problems. This group had the lowest levels of positive engagement in tasks with mothers.
- *Attention problems (10%).* This group had some attention problems and average cognitive and social skills.

- *Low cognitive ability (7%)*. This group scored lowest on cognitive measures and had average social skills and mild attention problems.

On the basis of these results, Konold and Pianta (2005) argued that there is more than one route to doing well in school. For example, their results showed that children with better cognitive functioning achieved adequately even if they were not functioning well socially. In other words, cognitive strengths might compensate for social skill deficits or problem behavior, and social strengths might compensate for poorer cognitive skills.

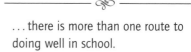

... there is more than one route to doing well in school.

However, they stressed that these "readiness" profiles of preschoolers only accounted for their first-grade performance to a small extent. From a child × environment perspective, they encourage us to attend to the ways in which adults enhance children's competencies *throughout* the early grades of school.

READINESS OF THE TEACHER

In the study reported earlier, Duncan and his colleagues (2007) concluded by emphasizing the potential for productive interventions during the early grades of school, and they suggested that "play-based" as opposed to "drill-and-practice" curricula "designed with the developmental needs of children in mind can foster the development of academic and attention skills in ways that are engaging and fun" (pp. 1443–1444). They referred to the *Big Math for Little Kids* program as an example (Greenes, Ginsburgh, & Balfanz, 2004; see Section II). In this section, we look at how some early school practices influence children's developing competencies, especially regulatory skills and learning approaches that further their adjustment and later learning.

Some early education programs are designed with the explicit goal of fostering children's self-regulation, such as those inspired by Maria Montessori (1966). The Montessori Method encourages children to make choices and manage their time in environments with a wide range of available activities. And research suggests that Montessori students demonstrate higher levels of self-regulation, independence, and initiative than those from traditional public schools. Research also shows that many public school teachers also value and believe young children are capable of self-directed learning, and importantly, implement constructivist (child-centered) practices associated with these goals (Stipek & Byler, 2004). In contrast, teachers who believe children less capable of self-directed learning engage in more didactic (teacher-centered) or traditional practices (see Chapter 1). Further, these different goals and practices are associated with corresponding child outcomes: Children in constructivist classrooms are more likely to demonstrate independence, persistence, and other behaviors indicating self-directed, positive approaches to learning than children in didactic classrooms (e.g., Stipek et al., 1998; Stipek, Feiler, Daniels, & Milburn, 1995). Similarly, children in classrooms with teachers who endorse learner-centered beliefs and practices show more positive motivational approaches than those in non-learner-centered classrooms (e.g., McCombs et al., 2008).

In sum, goals matter! Thus, *the first step for improving children's regulatory skills is to make child- or learner-centered practices a priority;* otherwise, other goals or external demands may take precedence, as Trudy (in the opening *Window*) discovered, and children may not develop essential skills and approaches for later school success.

The *second step is to create secure relationships in the classroom* as the base for children to pursue learning challenges with others they can count on for assistance and inspiration. Most developmental and educational psychologists point to the building of positive relationships, especially with teachers, as critical for children's learning and adjustment in the early years of school. Thus, we have devoted an entire chapter to this topic (Chapter 3).

The third obvious step is to implement effective practices. We might first look to what is happening in high quality, successful classrooms—like those described as child- or learner-centered or constructivist—to facilitate children's regulatory skills and learning approaches. Researchers have recently attended to influences of specific classroom practices. For example, Rimm-Kaufman et al. (2009) proposed that high quality classroom organizational practices would be the key contributor to children's adaptive behavior of concern here: self-control, engagement, and work habits. They also expected that these practices would be especially important for children who enter school with relatively low self-regulation skills (at risk for school failure), for example, boys and children lacking preschool experience. These researchers looked at three general aspects of management in kindergarten classrooms using the Classroom Assessment Scoring System (CLASS; Pianta, La Paro, & Hamre, 2008). (These types of organizational practices are also included in other major assessments of classroom quality, such as those used to identify child- or learner-centered practices.) One aspect of classroom management is teachers' ability to prevent and redirect children's misbehavior (*behavioral management*). The second factor is the extent to which teachers manage instructional time and routines so that appropriate learning opportunities are available (*productivity*). The third factor is how teachers use material and activities to facilitate learning opportunities (*instructional learning formats*). Recall that Trudy reported struggling with these last two aspects of classroom management; she identified problems early in the school year so that she could realize her goal to engage all of her students in important learning activities. (Chapter 4 attends to classroom management in more detail.)

Rimm-Kaufman and her colleagues (2009) found support for their first hypothesis. Children in particularly well-organized classrooms (i.e., teachers were productive, using varied instructional activities and proactive approaches to prevent misbehavior) showed greater engagement in learning activities and better (cognitive) self-control and work habits later in the school year. Surprisingly, they did not find evidence to support their second hypothesis: Children who entered school with less optimal self-regulatory and work habits were not influenced more. Instead, all children appeared to benefit similarly from high quality organizational practices. The authors explained that well-managed, high quality classroom experiences are probably critical for *all* children during this sensitive period of development for fostering self-control, positive work habits, and sustained engagement. They also proposed that children need boosts with sophisticated self-regulatory skills, such as planning and strategizing.

Thus, *the fourth step is to provide children with additional guidance when they plan and select strategies for learning tasks.* As seen in Chapter 1, children in the early years of school are able to develop simple plans and strategies for learning new material, but they often need hints to do so. For example, giving brief instructions can entice primary-grade children to use strategies, like rehearsing or categorizing lists of words to remember them, but providing explicit feedback is necessary to help young children realize which strategies are effective (Pressley & McCormick, 2007). In addition, teachers can encourage children to remember and plan (think backward and forward) by simply prompting, "what happened/ happens next?" or "what else did/can you do?" The *Tools of the Mind* program inspired by Vygotsky's theoretical ideas has made nurturing children's self-regulation and planning a goal (Bodrova & Leong, 2007). This program is considered an exemplary model for constructive teaching in preschool and the primary grades based on contemporary views of child development (Hyson et al., 2006). (See Chapter 4 and Resources.)

> Although some children may appear to enter school more ready than others, important self-regulatory skills are still "under construction" and need deliberate attention in elementary school.

Summary: Fostering Self-Regulatory Skills

To reiterate what has been established in this section so far—children continue to develop important "school readiness" skills in preschool and throughout the primary grades. Although some children may appear to enter school more ready than others, important self-regulatory skills are still "under construction" and need deliberate attention in elementary school. Children need opportunities, guidance, and practice directing their own learning among sensible and stimulating options. Fortunately, research shows that teachers can foster children's regulatory skills and positive approaches to learning through (a) understanding children's capabilities and making self-regulation a goal in the classroom; (b) promoting positive relationships; (c) establishing high quality, constructivist management practices; and (d) using effective guidance techniques, adapted for use with individual children. Unfortunately, national studies indicate that these kinds of practices may not be widespread in classrooms today (e.g., NICHD ECCRN, 2002, 2005). Recommendations for accomplishing b and c are provided in Chapters 3 and 4, respectively. Recommendations for effective guidance are included in Table 2.2.

CHILDREN AT RISK FOR ADJUSTMENT DIFFICULTIES

Some children come to school with qualities that present extra challenges for their adjustment. We focus on two here: children with excessive aggressive behavior and children with excessive withdrawn behavior. Teachers do not have any difficulty identifying children with overt behavioral problems such as aggression. These children are often topics of conversation in teacher lunchrooms as well as in more formal communications between teachers about children making grade transitions. However, teachers sometimes do have difficulty identifying children with less obvious displays of social anxieties (i.e., shyness) or withdrawn behavior. Preschool and primary teachers must work hard with other school professionals to help children regulate these tendencies because excessive behaviors may lead them toward peer rejection, academic problems, and difficult trajectories throughout school. Of course, it is common for children to display occasional aggressive or inhibited

Table 2.2   Promoting Self-Regulation in Preschool and
Primary-Grade Classrooms

Emotional Regulation (ER)

- Be a role model for how to express and regulate emotions, such as calming down before reacting or seeking help when frustrated.
- Encourage children to label emotions and identify causes and consequences of emotions in everyday activities.
- Discuss emotions with children. Label and identify causes and consequences of emotions during class meetings (circle times) and story discussions. (Many lessons, books, and props are available.)
- Intentionally instruct children in how to handle emotions. These strategies might include using self-talk to calm down, reframing the problem, identifying alternative actions, seeking help from others, and avoiding problem situations.
- Use validated methods designed to help children control negative emotions. Encourage children to relax, reflect on feelings, and then decide how to react to the cause of their feelings (see Resources for sources).
- Get involved in dramatic and role-playing activities with children.

Cognitive and Behavioral Regulation (Executive Function EF and Effortful Control EC)

- Provide a variety of learning activities that are challenging, meaningful, and require active participation.
- Involve children in establishing clear guidelines for classroom behavior and consistently apply these guidelines.
- Encourage children's self-talk to guide behavior (i.e., compliment themselves) and solve academic problems.
- Implement discovery-based learning.
- Allow children to derive and share multiple ways of solving academic problems (e.g., addition, manipulating objects and estimating).

Self-Directed Learning (Planning, Goal Setting, Strategy Use)

- Give children increasing responsibility for conducting challenging work on their own or with classmates.
- Let children design or choose how to complete some learning tasks.
- Ask children to talk about their plans in advance, using prompts like "what else . . ." and "remember when . . ." to connect to previous scripts for completing tasks.
- Support children's independent learning efforts.
- Help children set realistic, short-term goals and provide feedback about their progress.
- Provide specific information about strategies to remember, plan, and improve their work.
- Encourage autonomous help-seeking behavior. Provide hints, cues, or questions to assist after children have tried on their own (expert scaffolding).
- Help children figure out when they do and do not have the skills and resources to accomplish tasks.
- Create opportunities for children to engage in "reciprocal teaching," taking turns with the teacher and classmates to model the task process.

Responsible Decision Making (Social Behavior)

- Help children solve problems and make decisions by identifying issues (e.g., fair play on the playground), generating goals to guide decisions, thinking of alternative solutions and consequences, selecting the best solution, and making final plans (Kress & Elias, 2006).
- Refer to validated methods for social problem solving; check the Collaborative for Academic, Social, and Emotional Learning (CASEL) organization.

Sample Exemplary Programs: Second Step, Responsive Classroom Programs, Promoting Alternative Thinking Strategies (PATHS), Olweus Bullying Prevention Program, Tools for Thinking (see Resources).

behavior, especially when making adjustments to new settings. We are concerned about children who continue to show signs of aggressive and withdrawn behavior. These tendencies may be partly explained by their inherited temperaments, family experiences, and a host of other factors, including the school environment and experiences with classmates and peers.

Children With Aggressive Tendencies

Children who demonstrate **reactive aggression** are of concern because this type of aggression is associated with later peer rejection and victimization (e.g., Dodge, Lochman, Harnish, Bates, & Pettit, 1997). In contrast, children who engage in *proactive* aggression typically use aggression to meet a goal, such as obtaining a desired toy from another child. Reactively aggressive children do not seek to meet goals; instead, they are easily irritated and provoked and respond negatively to perceived or actual threats. They tend to incorrectly believe that others have acted hostilely toward them. Researchers have shown that aggressive children have trouble with many steps of social information processing (e.g., Dodge, Laird, Lochman, Zelli, & Conduct Problems Prevention Research Group, 2002). For example, aggressive children *encode* fewer relevant cues about a situation (Step 1) and *interpret* these cues differently (Step 2), with a bias toward overestimating hostility in others and underestimating their own so that they feel justified in blaming others for their aggressive acts. In the third step, *identifying social goals*, aggressive children tend to rate goals of revenge and self-protection higher than prosocial affiliation goals and constructive problem solving (Erdley & Asher, 1996). They also show limited abilities to *generate possible solutions;* for example, they are more likely to suggest seeking adult help or responding with physical aggression, and they are less likely to suggest verbal assertion or compromise. In the fifth step, *evaluating solutions*, aggressive children are more likely to view aggression as appropriate than nonaggressive children. Finally, in the sixth step of *enacting the behavior of the chosen response*, aggressive children have difficulty implementing positive and prosocial behaviors. For example, they may fail to convey their desires in a confident manner with appropriate body language, thus their peers may reject their verbal assertions. So children prone to aggression need help with each of these steps. Not surprisingly, children have less difficulty with all of these social information processing steps if they can calm their anger and other negative feelings (regulate their emotions).

Identifying problems can lead to solutions. Table 2.2 includes suggestions for helping children regulate their emotions and decision-making processes as well as program models for guidance. However, Izard (2002) pointed out that the "stop-and-think" techniques used in many successful prevention programs (traffic signs are actually used to remind children to STOP before reacting to anger) may not work as well with children who are very impulsive. These children may need simple, behaviorally oriented tools. For example, children may need to be redirected to a benign activity to reduce their anger first and then be engaged in a constructive problem-solving activity that includes considering feelings of others and appropriate self-assertion behaviors. Programs have also been designed to reduce aggression problems in children 4 to 8 years in particular, such as *The Incredible Years* program (e.g., Webster-Stratton, Reid, & Hammond, 2004). This program includes a teacher training component to build classroom management skills. Teachers can implement effective management practices such as those described in this book to reduce children's aggression toward their classmates. In addition, teachers can also limit aggressive children's interactions with other aggressive children who serve to maintain or escalate these behaviors. Raver et al. (2007) also suggested that teachers attend to how their own feelings and stressors influence their interactions with children, and they recommended that schools incorporate mental health consultants to help teachers with stress management so that they can develop positive relationships with children and provide positive models for them. These suggestions may be particularly important for teachers to work effectively with aggressive children and avoid developing conflicted relationships with them (see Chapter 3).

Children With Inhibited or Withdrawn Tendencies

Developmental and educational psychologists have also attended to ways of helping "shy" or socially withdrawn children adjust to school. Shy children tend to feel insecure or anxious in new social situations; they *want* to interact with others but are inhibited by fear and anxiety (unlike introverted children who may be content playing and working by themselves). Of course, many children exhibit shyness when entering a new school or classroom, but most become more comfortable within a week or so. Shyness is a problem when it continuously prevents children from engaging in social activities that they would like to take part in, and it may become stable over the years and lead to social, emotional, and adjustment difficulties (e.g., Coplan & Arbeau, 2008). Like some aggressive children, shy children *react* more extremely to situations, in this case novel social situations; this reaction may be partly explained by biological and environmental factors. In the classroom, temperamentally shy children speak less and display more **reticent behavior** (approach-avoidant behavior often manifested in prolonged onlooker behavior) than other children throughout the day; this lack of participation may encourage teachers to perceive them as less interested and intelligent and, in turn, provide fewer challenging learning opportunities for them. Shy children also tend to form more dependent, "clingy" relationships with teachers (e.g., Rudasill, Rimm-Kaufman, Justice, & Pence, 2006) associated with less adaptive classroom behavior (approaches to learning). Perhaps most important, these children have fewer opportunities to develop essential social skills during the early school years. Research also shows that if shy children are excluded from peer activities in kindergarten, they are more likely to remain shy and withdrawn over time (Gazelle & Ladd, 2003). Shy boys, in particular, are more prone to adjustment difficulties than shy girls, perhaps reflecting greater social acceptance of shyness for girls than boys in Western cultures (Coplan & Arbeau, 2008).

The good news is that shy children are not destined to have adjustment difficulties, and teachers can make a difference. Research indicates that teachers who form close (not dependent) relationships with shy children (see Chapter 3) and create positive classroom climates (see Chapter 4) buffer them from social difficulties. Teachers can provide opportunities for shy children to develop friendships to further protect them from adjustment problems (Rubin, Bukowski, & Parker, 2006). Once teachers have established a secure base through positive relations in encouraging classroom climates, they can consider the following suggestions from research to help children become less inhibited in the early grades of school (Coplan & Arbeau, 2008, pp. 382–384):

- Encourage children to speak more often through subtle and less controlling conversational forms (i.e., indirect personal comments: "I like ____," "hmmm . . . "), and use the same "wait time" for responses from all children.
- Play games in which children are required to take speaking turns, and subtly praise (e.g., by smiling) shy children for speaking.
- Encourage gradual participation in class discussions by asking shy children questions they can respond to (even if it is just their names).
- Establish personal relationships with shy children by having private conversations with them about their families or out-of-school experiences.
- Gently encourage shy children to interact with other children in the classroom; one can start by pairing them with more sociable classmates.
- Prepare shy children for changes in the routine or special events.

Other researchers suggest that shy children are helped by the following:

- Participation in cross-age tutoring and play groups
- Interactions in thoughtfully designed cooperative learning groups in the classroom

Shy children will benefit from many of the strategies to encourage self-regulation as well. *The Child's Window* provides a view of a potentially shy child's life in the classroom.

The Child's Window

Hector is in the second month of kindergarten. He is one of the older 5-year-olds and a little bigger than most of the other children in Trudy's class (see the opening Window Into Practice). When I first observed Hector, he was sitting quietly in his small group working independently on a prereading assignment. There was a low hum of children's voices and activities surrounding him. He attended to his work, occasionally looking up to observe those around him. When Trudy called the children to the rug for story time, he quickly put his materials away and joined the group. He appeared attentive to the story, but I didn't see him smile or respond in any way to the teacher's questions. He didn't stand out; some of the other children also just quietly listened. When they were finished, he followed the children to the door to go outside for recess. On the playground, Hector hung around the swing area, apparently waiting for a turn. I did not observe him talk or interact with other children. Hector did not stand out; several other children from his class also appeared not to be engaged in activities, perhaps because the playground was so large and had few materials geared for their age. When the bell rang, Hector quickly lined up to return to class. During the next classroom activity—an art activity related to the story just read—Hector waited to begin his drawing until the teacher assistant showed him what to do. Although he appeared to be listening to the children's quiet chatter around him, he did not participate in the conversation. Toward the end of this activity, I asked him if he would like to talk with me for a few minutes about school. He nodded and followed me to a chair nearby in the listening center. He responded quietly to my questions, sometimes averting my gaze, but he did not appear to be fearful or anxious (he appeared more reluctant to return to his seat when we were finished). He smiled sweetly a couple of times during the Heads-to-Toes "game" I played with him to assess his behavioral regulation. He responded positively to most of the questions I asked him. He thought his teacher liked him and that he could do most kindergarten activities well, but he couldn't decide whether he liked school a little or not, and he did not respond at first to my prompts about what he did and did not like. After a minute or so, he said that he liked to do "other things better." Hector didn't stand out; many kindergarteners hesitate or respond with "I don't know" to questions concerning their feelings about school. Trudy rated Hector as "average" in his adjustment to kindergarten across the board—in his behavioral conduct, social skills, preacademic skills, and participation in class activities. Hector didn't stand out.

Thankfully, Hector was one of the children on Trudy's "radar" for getting to know better. He might not have been seen at all in other classrooms. Hector may or may not be temperamentally shy, but he is showing enough signs of nonparticipatory behavior (and less optimal learning approaches) to warrant extra attention.

READINESS OF THE SCHOOL

Fostering Transitions

So far we have focused on readying children for school and teachers for children in the early grades. In this section, we return to the larger ecological model and take a brief look at *readying schools for children* and making connections between the home, preschool, and elementary school. Creating coherent connections between these major contexts in young children's lives leads to stability in relationships and consistency in information-sharing—especially between preschool and kindergarten teachers, and teachers and parents—to promote their early adaptation and school success. The National Education Goals Panel (NEGP) of advisors (1998) identified 10 characteristics of *ready schools*. The first two characteristics are relevant here:

1. Ready schools smooth the transition between home and school.

2. Ready schools strive for continuity between early care and education programs and elementary schools.

Psychologists, educators, and policymakers are seeking ways to establish school connections that prove to be effective in fostering children's early adjustment. Some researchers have attended to how preschool teachers can create a "bridge of support" for children as they transition to kindergarten. For example, LoCasale-Crouch, Mashburn, Downer, and Pianta (2008) examined the use of the following common practices:

- Prekindergarten children visit a kindergarten class.
- The prekindergarten teacher visits a kindergarten class.
- The kindergarten teacher visits a preschool class.
- The school holds a spring kindergarten orientation for prekindergarten children.
- The school holds a spring kindergarten orientation for prekindergarten children's parents.
- There is a schoolwide activity for prekindergarten children.
- Teachers hold individual meetings with parents about kindergarten.
- Teachers share written records about children's prekindergarten experience with the elementary school.
- Teachers contact the kindergarten teacher about curriculum and/or specific children.

Importantly, these researchers not only examined if these practices were used but how they influenced children's adjustment and competencies when they entered kindergarten (i.e., self-regulatory, social, literacy skills). They found that preschool teachers reported implementing a wide range of practices (an average of six); the most frequent was sharing written records, and the least frequent was having kindergarten teachers visit their classes. Interestingly, contact between preschool and kindergarten teachers about curriculum or a specific child was the one practice most strongly and consistently associated with children's positive adjustment in kindergarten. Children who experienced more transitional practices (especially those directly involved) were seen as better adjusted by their kindergarten teachers; this was particularly the case for children with social and economic risk factors.

These findings are consistent with findings from a large national study examining the use of transition practices implemented by kindergarten teachers at the beginning of the year: More transition practices were associated with better adaptation and achievement of children, especially those from lower income families (Schulting, Malone, & Dodge, 2005). Thus, the use of transition practices has the potential to improve outcomes for children at risk for poor adjustment to school. The next chapter highlights home-school connections and development of positive relationships between teachers, parents, and children to further these goals.

The major points regarding transition practices are:

1. Teacher-to-teacher talk about children and curriculum across schools and grade levels matters.

2. Preschool and kindergarten teachers' use of several different transitional activities pays off; all children benefit.

3. Involving children in these activities pays off.

4. Children at risk for poor school adjustment especially benefit from involvement in transitional activities.

Further, use of transition practices should facilitate alignment of educational practices across the grades from preschool through third (PK–3); such alignment has been advocated for improving children's success and buffering them from failure in school (Bogard & Takanishi, 2005; Pianta et al., 2007). Several community school readiness models are currently

... researchers and educators view school readiness as an extended transition process that begins before school entry and continues throughout the early elementary years and beyond.

available for demonstrating how to link teachers, children, and parents between schools (see Resources).

Although we have focused on the transition from preschool to kindergarten, many researchers and educators view school readiness as an extended transition process that begins before school entry and continues throughout the early elementary years and beyond. This view of the transition process "recognizes that children, families, and teachers all need to adapt to and understand one another so that children will like school and be able to benefit from the experience" (Ramey & Ramey, 1994, p. 195). This view stems from contemporary perspectives on children's development and specifically that all children are eager to learn and make progress when they are in classrooms and school environments that are tailored to their developmental skills and needs. Children are particularly vulnerable when they first enter a new classroom and have different needs than they do once they have adjusted. The following section exposes young children's views of school at different points in this transition process.

Children's Views of School
Preschool Through Third Grade

Weinstein (2002) argued that the "voices of the primary consumers of education are largely unheard," that children's views of their experiences in school are "virtually absent" (p. 91). This is not the case when educators embrace learner-centered approaches advocated by the American Psychological Association (APA) and based on contemporary perspectives of children's learning and development (see Chapter 1). Professional development activities associated with learner-centered approaches often begin with revealing students' perceptions of classroom practices to their teachers (e.g., McCombs & Whisler, 1997). Students' perspectives are essential to obtain if we want to better understand how to improve their motivation and learning in school. Even children in the primary grades provide valuable information about their school experiences that are sensibly linked to their motives and approaches to learning in classrooms (McCombs et al., 2008). Indeed, research indicates that simply asking children how much they like kindergarten soon after entering may help to predict their participation in class activities and subsequent achievement (Ladd, Buhs, & Seid, 2000).

Children's views can even be gathered before they enter school. For example, a few months prior to kindergarten, we asked a number of children in local preschools to predict how much they would like kindergarten and explain why (they were to attend more than a dozen different schools). As anticipated, most children were optimistic and expected to like kindergarten either "a lot" or "pretty much"; others were not so sure. A few of our favorite explanations follow: "I want to find out how much I weigh," "I want to go on the monkey bars with the teachers," and "It will be like getting shots." Some expressed concerns with having homework. One particularly astute child stated, "I won't like it much at first. Nope. But I will later. . . ." Importantly, children's expectations for liking kindergarten were related to their teachers' ratings of their adjustment to school soon after they entered (Daniels, 2009). Hence, we have good reason to ask and listen to young children's views of school.

In interviews with primary-grade children, several themes emerge regarding their perspectives on good teachers and important classroom practices (Daniels & Perry, 2003). First, they want their teachers to care and support them as individuals ("She looks at me and smiles."). Second, children want their teachers to provide interesting and appropriately challenging learning opportunities (e.g., "She teaches me a lot."); some are particularly repulsed by repetitive, boring worksheets and assessments ("Tests hardly make me think!") and work that they don't understand how to do ("It's hard to do what she asks . . ."). Third, children, particularly in Grades 2 and above, want to be able to choose their activities on occasion (" . . . ask what ideas we'd like to do."). Fourth, children want to work with their classmates ("We can work with others and give a clue."); they are especially concerned when they have limited opportunities to do so ("We do our own problems, but if we sneak . . ."). Although simple, children's views are remarkably consistent with expert views of effective classroom practices (learner-centered, developmentally appropriate practice) that meet children's basic psychological needs for relatedness, autonomy, and competence (self-determination theory; Ryan & Deci, 2000).

CHAPTER SUMMARY

We began this chapter with a glimpse into a kindergarten classroom that would be considered fairly high quality and developmentally appropriate by childhood experts. And expectedly, most children were well-adjusted, but not all. From a child × environment perspective, we understand that children are continuing to develop "readiness" qualities throughout the early years in schools that are more or less ready to nurture them. We looked at characteristics of children, such as their age, temperament (i.e., shyness), regulatory skills, and approaches to learning, and the influences on school adjustment. We also made recommendations for enhancing self-regulation skills essential for optimal functioning and well-being in school, as well as additional suggestions to help some children at risk for poor adjustment. We ventured outside the classroom a bit to look at ways schools can foster the important transition from preschool or home to school. Finally, we returned to viewing school from children's perspectives to help us better understand their adjustment problems and potentials. Our hope is that such insights from research will enhance children's early school adjustment.

Questions to Ponder

1. How do think that your own emotional regulation (ER) and effortful control (EC) skills have affected your approaches to learning in school?

2. How do think that your ER and EC skills affect your interactions with children in general or with aggressive

or shy children? How does stress interfere with these processes? What kinds of supports bolster your attempts to interact in positive ways with children?

Practice Exercises

1. **Revealing Children's EC Skills in "Opposite Games."** Play a game that requires children to resist a dominant response. For example, ask them to play a "pencil tapping" game by instructing them to tap once when you tap twice and vice versa. Or play a "heads-to-toes" game by asking children to touch their toes when you ask them to touch their heads and vice versa. Are children able to briefly "stop and think" to regulate their behavior? You can make it more challenging and fun for older children by adding more taps or body parts to the game. Researchers have used games like these (with detailed instructions) to assess children's effortful control (EC) or behavioral regulation (e.g., Ponitz et al., 2008; Rimm-Kaufman et al., 2009). You might be able to glean some clues about children's EC skills from simple games like these.

2. **Observe Children's Approaches to Learning.** Check Table 2.1 for behaviors indicating positive approaches to learning in the classroom. Observe one or two children for several hours in their preschool or primary-grade classrooms and note examples of these behaviors. To what extent did these children reveal positive approaches to learning? What behaviors indicated negative approaches? What classroom practices do you think tended to foster positive approaches? How might these practices and approaches affect children's school learning?

3. **Interview Children About Their Feelings About School.** Ask familiar children to tell you how much they like school. You can provide a "face scale" for young children to choose their response: draw four faces representing "very much" (big smile), "pretty much" (little smile), "just a little" (straight face), or "not

at all" (big frown). Ask them to explain: "Why did you say that you liked school _____?" You can ask a number of related questions using this format, such as how much they like particular activities, the teacher, and so forth. Be sure to consider your role and ethical issues when asking such questions; we recommend only asking children you are familiar with (and outside your own class).

Key Words

School readiness

School adjustment

Domains of readiness

Self-regulation

Executive function (EF)

Effortful control (EC)

Emotional regulation (ER)

Approaches to learning

Profiles of school readiness

Reactive aggression

Reticent behavior

3

The Primacy of Relationships in the Early School Years

Fostering Relationships

Window Into Practice

Brandi had been a preschool teacher for over 10 years. She had been teaching in the PreK program for most of that time. The preschool's philosophy and mission statement reflected a desire to partner with parents in the education and development of their children. Parent conferences were held once a year and most parents participated. In addition, the preschool holiday programs and graduation ceremonies were well-attended by parents, grandparents, and neighbors. As a teacher, Brandi made sure that she wrote notes about potential issues and problems with children, many times speaking to parents in person at drop-off or pick-up times. Brandi felt good about her efforts to maintain a partnership with the parents of the children in her class, and she felt that parents were generally happy with her communication as well. Much to Brandi's surprise, a parent survey revealed otherwise. Several parents reported that although they felt their children were in a nurturing environment, there was something lacking in the communication and sense of "partnership" between the parents and the teachers. In the survey, parents noted that they missed some of their children's developmental milestones during school hours. The preschool staff had made efforts to communicate through all of the major events, but there was a lack of communication regarding daily activities in children's lives that were important to parents. One parent described her feelings as trying to watch your child in a championship game through a small hole in a wooden fence. Her view of her child was narrow and limited to the scope of the hole (i.e., holiday programs, conferences, infrequent small talks with the teacher).

Brandi, along with several of her colleagues, reflected on these comments and reevaluated their efforts for parent involvement. One of their conclusions was that the "involvement" had been only one way (teacher to parent) and that they had not really considered what channels of communication parents would prefer, what information parents would desire, and how they could foster a true partnership of two-way communication. Together with her colleagues, Brandi drafted another parent survey to ask more questions. After reading the responses, teachers made some changes in their practice of "partnership." Expanding the analogy of the "hole in the fence view," the teachers drafted activities that would create a "chain-linked fence view" for parents. This open fence would provide a view for parents which not only visually represented more of the whole game (children's daily experiences and milestones), but it would also allow parents to participate at their level of availability and comfort. The practical activities and practices Brandi and her colleagues collected included a wide variety of communication avenues. The teachers planned to provide digital pictures of individual children engaged in specific activities that could be used to tell parents a "story" about their child's day or skill development. Digital recordings of children's voices could also be used to narrate some of the thoughts about the event. This would help parents "feel like they were there" and experience school with their children. E-mail could also provide positive home interactions between parents and children about school and learning. Next, the teachers decided to personally call parents at home once a quarter to check in, offer support, and convey positive aspects of their child's growth and development. This would help alleviate the notion that phone calls home are "always about negative behavior." It would also help to get to know children better. The next plan was to use "Skype" with parents who had access to a computer webcam; parents could view and converse with their child in "real time" during the day, possibly taking part in a special party or activity as it was happening. For families with limited access to computers, teachers decided to produce photographs of children and brief descriptions of their daily activities. Brandi and her colleagues committed to following through with these ideas for the next 6 months and then reevaluate their effectiveness by taking another survey of parents' feelings about their involvement and communication.

Brandi employed traditional parental involvement methods that needed improvement. Parent surveys revealed gaps in communication and involvement that inspired teachers to develop specific action plans for improvement. Studies show that parental involvement encourages children's positive attitudes toward school, greater motivation to learn, and enhanced learning. Parental involvement activities are most effective when complemented by a true "partnership" relationship between teacher and parent, which also serve to improve teacher-child relationships.

This chapter focuses on the development of positive relationships or partnerships in the early years of school that are vital for children's adjustment, learning, and achievement. We begin with arguments made by major developmental psychologists and educators for this perspective and approach to school reform. We then point to research documenting the importance of relationships between (a) teachers and children, (b) children and their peers, and (c) teachers and parents. Furthermore, we note how children's relationships with teachers, parents, and peers influence one another (see Figure 3.1). Within each of these sections, we make recommendations for promoting positive relationships and partnerships based on research. These relationships provide the foundation for establishing positive classroom climates discussed further in the next chapter. Finally, we return to suggestions for fostering home-school connections and parental involvement in school.

SCHOOL REFORM MODELS

Fostering Positive Relationships Is Key

From contemporary developmental perspectives, relationships in school not only matter because they influence children's adjustment and learning, the quality of these relationships may be *the* best indicator of later school success

The simple idea here is that children cannot learn well unless they feel secure in their environment, and these feelings stem from their relationships with others.

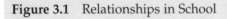

Figure 3.1   Relationships in School

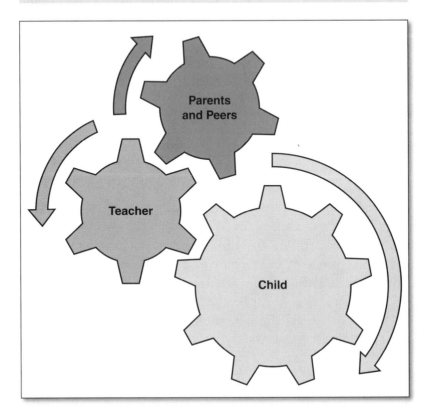

and well-being (Rimm-Kaufman & Pianta, 2000). Relationships between teachers and children, children and children, and teachers and parents may become patterned in the early years and affect later relationships, thus placing children on stable pathways through school. Thus, it is imperative to create quality relationships that direct children toward positive pathways. This focus on relationships is the motto of successful school reform efforts, such as the School Development Program, inspired by child psychiatrist, James Comer (2004). He argued that "good relationships make student, adult, and organizational development possible, which, in turn, makes a strong academic focus possible" (p. xiv). The development of relationship skills in schools is also central in other major organizational efforts to improve schools through research-to-practice connections, such as the Collaborative for Academic, Social, and Emotional Learning (CASEL), the National Association for the Education of Young Children (NAEYC), and the APA Center for Psychology in Schools and Education (CPSE) and promotion of learner-centered practices for school reform (e.g., Lambert & McCombs, 1998). Information about programs and organizations committed to creating caring relationships in schools is provided in Resources. These school reformers intentionally respond to children's basic needs for relatedness, as well as for autonomy and competence, based on psychological theories and research (e.g., Ryan & Deci, 2000). The simple idea here is that children cannot learn well unless they feel secure in their environment, and these feelings stem from their relationships with others.

TEACHER-CHILD RELATIONSHIPS

Teacher-child relationships play a formative role in children's self-regulation and academic skills in the early years of school (Pianta, 1999, 2004) and continue to forecast their later adjustment and achievement through eighth grade (Hamre & Pianta, 2001). Although children's earlier relationships with caregivers and regulatory skills (Valiente et al., 2008) may make forming positive relationships with them more or less challenging, studies suggest that sensitive, involved teachers can overcome difficulties and make a profound difference in redirecting children toward positive trajectories through school (NICHD ECCRN, 2005). Sensitive teachers are those that provide emotional support for children; they are adults to count on for understanding and guidance. Teacher-child relationships can be described in terms of their *affection* (i.e., how much the teacher likes and enjoys the child), *attunement* (i.e., the extent to which the teacher understands, sympathizes with, and knows the child), and *dependability* (i.e., the teacher's availability when needed; Skinner & Belmont, 1993). Research indicates that many teachers in the United States have positive relationships with children in their classrooms, and some do not.

The quality of teacher-child relationships can also be characterized in the following ways (sample items from the

Student-Teacher Relationship Scale are included in parentheses; Pianta, 1999):

- *Close.* Teacher and child share a warm relationship, openly communicate about personal items, appear comfortable with appropriate dependency, and display positive affect. (For example, "I share an affectionate, warm relationship with this child"; "If upset, this child will seek comfort from me"; "This child spontaneously shares information about himself/herself.")
- *Conflicted.* Teacher and child are often angry and at odds with each other, little warmth and personal communication is displayed, and they appear to be disconnected. Teachers often feel troubled by their inability to "reach" these children. (For example, "This child easily becomes angry at me"; "This child and I always seem to be struggling with each other.")
- *Dependent.* Child "clings" to teacher and asks for help when unnecessary; interactions with teacher are often emotionally negative. (For example, "This child reacts strongly to separation from me"; "This child is overly dependent on me.")

Of course, relationships can also be described in other ways, including "mixes" of the characteristics described earlier. As noted in Chapter 2, children with aggressive tendencies are prone to having **conflicted relationships,** and children with shyness tendencies are prone to having **dependent relationships** with teachers. It is no surprise that children with closer relationships with teachers fare better in school than children with negative relationships marked by conflict or overdependency. For example, Birch and Ladd (1997) found that children who shared a **close relationship** with their teacher demonstrated greater academic performance, school attitudes, and engagement in school activities (i.e., self-directed learning, cooperative participation) than children experiencing conflict or dependency. Researchers assume that close relationships provide children with felt security and positive feelings to boost their learning and confidence, allowing them to pursue further challenges.

Children's relationships with teachers may be patterned after their earlier relationships with caregivers (e.g., Pianta, 2004); thus, children with secure relationships may expect and elicit positive responses from other adults that serve to perpetuate close relationships, and children with prior insecure relationships may be more likely to expect and evoke negative responses which perpetuate dependent or conflicted relationships. Fortunately, teachers can circumvent negative cycles, but it may not be easy. Studies have shown that negative relationships with teachers in the earlier grades are sometimes perpetuated at the next grade level (Howes, Phillipsen, & Peisner-Feinberg, 2000). Consistent with **attachment theory** formulated by John Bowlby (1969), Howes and her colleagues proposed that children form mental or **working models** of relationships with earlier teachers that may lead them to expect future teachers to be positive (i.e., trustworthy, helpful) or negative; thus, they behave in ways that fulfill their expectations (Howes, Hamilton, & Phillipsen, 1998). The goal is to help children become appropriately dependent; this takes patience and perseverance. When children have not developed a sense of trust, they might test teachers' intentions many times. Because they also may not have developed age-appropriate social and emotional competencies in earlier relationships, they might display more emotional outbursts and harm others, making it even more difficult for teachers to like them.

Teachers can reflect on their relationships with individual children by asking themselves some of the questions researchers ask to characterize teacher-child relationships. For example, Table 3.1 includes sample questions from the Teacher Relationship Interview (TRI) developed by Pianta and his colleagues. Researchers consider themes as well as the affective tone of responses.

Pianta (1999) and other developmental psychologists provide several recommendations for enhancing relationships between teachers and children in the early grades. First, as we discussed in Chapter 2, it is important to encourage emotional

Table 3.1   Sample Questions From the Teacher Relationship Interview

1. Choose three words that describe your relationship with _____ *child's name.*

   For each word, tell me a specific experience or time that describes that word.

2. Tell me about a specific time you can think of when you and ___ "clicked."

   How did you feel? How do you think _____ felt?

3. Tell me about a specific time you can think of when you and ____ really weren't "clicking."

4. What gives you the most satisfaction being _____'s teacher? Why?

5. Every teacher has at least occasional doubts about whether s/he is meeting a child's needs. What brings this up for you and ____? How do you handle these doubts?

6. What is your relationship like with _____'s family?

(Select items adapted from the Teacher Relationship Interview, Pianta, 1999.)

regulation. Second, it is important to organize the classroom schedule and activities to allow regular contact between the teacher and individual children, as well as design systems to prevent misbehavior (see Chapter 4). The value of having stable, predictable, and pleasant contacts between children and particular teachers cannot be overstated. Another recommendation is to implement a "Banking Time" intervention. This intervention is based on the notion that children must receive attention on an unconditional basis from the teacher. In other words, time needs to be built into the day so that the teacher can attend to each child. At the classroom level, teachers can arrange brief periods (e.g., 10 minutes) of Banking Time with small groups while engaged in child-chosen activities. Activities might include board games, arts and crafts, and interesting projects taken from the academic curriculum. Using this approach, a teacher can spend time with five or six children at a time, rotating groups so that during the course of a typical week, the teacher might be involved with each child two to three times. The following Banking Time principles apply: (a) Children are told that the time is theirs to do what they wish; teachers follow and participate as children direct; (b) the sessions occur on a predictable basis, and participation is *not* contingent on children's behavior; (c) the teacher is neutral and objective and does not focus on children's performance or skills; (d) the teacher draws attention to a few relationship messages (e.g., "I accept you," "You are important," "I am available," "I am consistent," "I am helpful when asked"). These messages convey the teacher as "... a helper, a person who is unconditionally available and predictable, a source of safety and comfort, and a resource for problem solving ... common to most child-teacher relationships" (Pianta, 1999, p. 141). With consistent implementation over time, such messages will convey the experienced teacher-child relationship and override situational stressors.

Perhaps most important for reducing negative interactions with children, teachers need to reflect on their own beliefs and feelings. They should try to avoid a "within child" view of their relationships with children (Erikson & Pianta, 1989). This means that instead of thinking of children as "aloof," "clingy," or "mean," consider how children may have developed ways of interacting with others that need reworking in new relationships. Teachers also need to consider how they might inadvertently be perpetuating negative relationships with some children. Such awareness may involve reflecting on how their own earlier relationships impact their interactions with children. A few studies indicate that teachers with secure relationships (i.e.,

Teachers also need to consider how they might inadvertently be perpetuating negative relationships with some children.

with their own parents) view their relationships with children more positively than those with less secure relationships (e.g., Pianta, 2004). Teachers also need to attend to their current emotional experiences as well, such as stress (see previous chapter) and depression (Hamre & Pianta, 2004), and look for means of support for themselves.

Creating a supportive context for teachers to support children's development is a cornerstone of Comer's School Development Program (SDP) implemented in schools across the country (Comer, 2004). In this program, social problems in the classroom are sometimes solved with the assistance of helping professionals in a school (e.g., social workers, special educator teachers, other health professionals) on the Student and Staff Support Team. One of the key operating principles of this team is "no-fault" problem solving: neither the child nor the teacher are blamed for problematic interactions; instead, adults in the school focus on how to solve the problem together. Teachers feel supported in this positive school climate and thus are better able to deal positively and effectively with children. Some SDP teams have decided to implement a looping system in their schools so that after teachers have worked hard to establish positive relationships with children, they can benefit for another year together. Sustaining positive teacher-child relationships for several years has also been a major reason for instituting multigrade classrooms where team-teachers stay with the same group of children for 2 or more years. Other model programs for meeting teacher as well as student needs are described in Resources.

Simple survey questions have been developed for primary-grade children to assess their perspectives of relationships in the classroom, including with their teacher, such as in the K–3 Assessment of Learner-Centered Practices (ALCP; McCombs et al., 2008). Children's views of the extent to which their teacher created positive interpersonal relationships in the classroom were related to their perceptions of competence and interests in school learning. Importantly, children's views were more powerful than teachers' reports of classroom practices in predicting their motivation. Sample items from the ALCP are shown in Table 3.2. In professional

Table 3.2   Interpersonal Relations in the Classroom: Sample Items From the K–3 Student Assessment of Learner-Centered Practices (ALCP)

My teacher likes me.	
My teacher makes me feel like I am part of the class.	
My teacher helps me feel good about myself.	
My teacher helps me get along with the other kids in my class.	

(Adapted from McCombs, Daniels, & Perry, 2008.)

development programs, children's views (as a group) can be shared with teachers in efforts to promote their awareness and understanding of how their practices influence children.

Note that the last item on the table involves how teachers help children get along with one another. This is a very important feature of teacher-child relationships, and it is the focus of the next section.

Before moving onward, we highlight suggestions made so far for promoting positive teacher-child relationships:

- Reflect on individual relationships with children. Attend to those that may not yet be close or positive.
- Help children develop emotional regulation skills so that they are better able to form positive interpersonal relations with others, including teachers.
- Create frequent opportunities in classroom routines for positive teacher-child interactions that children can anticipate and count on.
- Ensure that individual children have regular "unconditional" opportunities to develop positive relationships with a stable teacher (employ "Banking Time").
- Consider how previous relationships or stressors affect relationships with children. Obtain support from mentors or other school professionals when needed.

Stipek (2002) added the following suggestions to foster positive relationships:

- Respect and value children as human beings; take their ideas seriously and show interest in their personal lives outside school.
- Expect positive behavior and work from children; hold them to developmentally appropriate standards.
- Ensure that children are not humiliated; avoid embarrassing or making sarcastic remarks about them (young children are likely to take remarks literally).
- Let children know that there is no risk of disapproval or rejection when they do poorly on their work; praise children when they attempt challenging tasks, even when they fail.

Positive teacher-child relationships also appear to be fostered in classrooms with developmentally appropriate practices (DAP or child/learner-centered; see Chapter 4). Stipek and her colleagues (e.g., Stipek et al., 1998; Stipek et al., 1995) found that teachers were more warm, nurturing, and attentive to individual children's needs in child-centered classrooms than in teacher-centered, didactic classrooms. One of the reasons for this connection may be that children are happier, better behaved, and more engaged in these types of classrooms, making it easier for everyone to get along with one another. Another reason might be that there is more time in DAP classrooms for teachers to interact with children in small groups or individually (e.g., "Banking Time") than in classrooms where the teacher is directing whole class activities; thus, teachers and children have more opportunities to get to know one another and develop closer relationships. Yet another reason is that teachers in DAP classrooms use less adult-imposed responses to misbehavior, such as time-out. Howes and Ritchie (2002) found that classrooms were more caring in nature when teachers used alternatives to time-out. Thus, our final suggestion for promoting positive teacher-child relationships is to implement DAP, introduced in the next chapter.

Teachers' relationships with children impact their peer relations. Children with higher quality relationships with their teachers demonstrate fewer behavioral problems (Hamre & Pianta, 2001) and greater social skills with their peers (Howes, Matheson, & Hamilton, 1994). Researchers have also shown that the nature and extent of a teacher's interactions with a child influences classmates' views of and affiliations with that child (Hughes, Cavell, & Wilson, 2001). *The Child's Window* depicts a child who continues to struggle with teacher and peer relationships in school. The importance of promoting positive peer relationships in the classroom is the topic of the next section.

The Child's Window

Katie is 7 years old. She doesn't like her new second-grade teacher. She has already been in "time-out" twice today for yelling and bothering the girl sitting next to her in class. "She isn't my friend," Katie shouted before she stomped off to the time-out chair. Katie scooted the chair over to the pencil sharpener and started playing with it; after tiring of that activity, she started making chirping noises. Mrs. Snow wouldn't look at her. Finally, the bell rang, and Katie lined up at the door with the rest of the children and ran for the swings on the playground. She was there first—GOOD—she stayed on the swing for a long time despite seeing the other children waiting for their turns. She got off reluctantly when the yard duty lady told her to. When she returned to class, Katie went to her reading group. She didn't mind reading time because she was able to work with the student teacher, Miss Jill, who was nice and helped her with the hard words. She knew that most of the other children in the class were reading longer books. She wished that she could do this too. She didn't want to leave to go to lunch next, but Miss Jill had to go home. Katie walked to the lunch room alone. As she was walking, she thought about first grade. She was happier there because John played with her, but she didn't like her first-grade teacher either. She heard her teacher say a couple of times that she was a "problem child." Her mom called her that too sometimes, or more often, "strong-willed" when she screamed to do something she wanted to do. This usually worked with her mom but not with her stepdad, who usually ignored her when he was there and paid attention to "his" children—her older stepbrothers—instead.

When Katie returned to class after lunch, her teacher told her that she was calling her parents for a conference so that they could work together to make Katie's life at school better. Uh-Oh! Mrs. Snow smiled, but Katie still felt uncomfortable.

CHILD-CHILD RELATIONSHIPS IN SCHOOL

Children's acceptance by their peers in the classroom is essential for their school adjustment and learning. In a recent study, Ladd, Herald-Brown, and Reiser (2008) found that children rejected by their peers in grades K–3 exhibited significantly lower levels of participation in class activities. Indeed, rejection was associated with both lower independent *and* cooperative classroom participation. One can see how Katie (in *The Child's Window*) might miss out on learning opportunities in the classroom, not just because she is left behind in "time-out," but also because her classmates are probably reluctant to work with her; she's not very considerate of others. In addition, she is falling behind her peers academically and is beginning to realize this, making it more difficult for her to be inspired to do schoolwork. On the bright side, however, Ladd and his colleagues found that children who transitioned from rejection to acceptance increased engagement in class activities. There is hope. Obviously, engagement in class is central to learning and achievement in school, and fostering acceptance of children by their peers in the classroom must be taken seriously for this reason as well as to enhance their general well-being. Rejection hurts, even if children appear not to care. Ladd and his colleagues proposed a number of explanations for the connection between peer rejection and participation in classroom learning. One is that feelings of pain and discomfort associated with rejection impair executive functioning in the brain (see Chapter 1). Thus, children may be less able to focus, concentrate, and learn because of this interference. Another explanation might simply be that rejected children participate less because they are ignored or excluded from more activities. And negative emotions associated with rejection, such as anxiety or sadness or insecurity, may reduce children's motivation to become involved and cause them to

> Engagement in class is central to learning and achievement in school, and fostering acceptance of children by their peers in the classroom must be taken seriously for this reason.

withdraw from challenging activities. In any case, it is clearly important for teachers to help children develop positive peer relations, feel accepted by their classmates, and learn to resolve social conflicts. These social competencies and relationships provide the foundation for a positive classroom climate (see Chapter 4).

However, Pellegrini and Blatchford (2000) warned that adults not become overly involved in children's peer relations. They argued on the basis of research and theory that children must work harder to engage their peers than adults and therefore develop better social competencies with moderate adult intervention. **Social competence** is defined as socially adaptive behavior. In early childhood, social adaptability with peers includes (a) the successful and positive seeking of peers' attention, (b) effectively using peers as resources, and (c) successfully leading peers. As we have seen, to accomplish these tasks, children also need to be able to manage their emotions and impulses. As children transition into middle childhood, they begin to develop more sophisticated perspective-taking and communication skills, allowing them to form and sustain close friendships and function in stable peer groups. Children are most likely to develop positive social competencies if they have been socialized in family and school contexts where adults are warm and nurturing, encourage independence, have clear expectations for mature behavior, but are not overly controlling—again, supporting a child- or learner-centered over an adult- centered approach.

Studies also show that high numbers of adults in early educational settings may inhibit social interaction with peers (e.g., Pellegrini & Blatchford, 2000). Interestingly, this particular perspective is embraced by teachers of young children in Japan where low teacher to child ratios are common (e.g., Lewis, 1995; Tobin, Hsueh, & Karasawa, 2009). Such findings are consistent with a Piagetian perspective that points to the importance of peer interactions for provoking children's cognitive and social development. With peers as equals, children must consider and accommodate different views (instead of merely accepting adult views). According to Pellegrini and Blatchford (2000), then, preschool and primary-grade school teachers also need to provide opportunities for children to interact with their peers with minimal adult direction. In particular, they suggest ensuring that children have opportunities for free play in the classroom and on the playground during recess and break times. The structure of the classroom matters too; they point to earlier research showing that children had more friends in relatively "open" multitask classrooms than in traditional, ability-grouped classroom settings. Friendships in elementary school are also facilitated in structured games on the playground (e.g., soccer).

Fostering friendships in school not only fosters children's adjustment (they like school and cope in school better) but their academic learning. Friends collaborate and solve academic problems more effectively than nonfriends, and perhaps surprisingly, spend less time off-task (e.g., Zajac & Hartup, 1997). A few studies even suggest that friends use more sophisticated cognitive processes when working on academic tasks. For example, researchers have found that 6-year-old friends were more likely to reflect on language (e.g., "How do you write ___?") and thought (e.g., "Try to put this one first.") processes when writing and talking about books than acquaintances in the same classroom (e.g., Pellegrini & Blatchford, 2000). These findings indicate that teachers should not always implement the common practice of separating friends in group activities. It is also important to note that not all friendships are positive; as noted in the previous chapter, there are good reasons for separating children with antisocial or aggressive tendencies.

Pellegrini and Blatchford (2000) concluded that there is much work that can be done within schools to foster social skills and friendships, but we also need to allow children opportunities to meet and sustain their interactions during recess and other times relatively free from adult control. They are very concerned about policies that restrict these occasions in elementary schools. Recess is a major part of school life for children (Pellegrini & Bohn, 2005). In fact, when children are asked about their day at school, their first responses often concern their activities at recess or lunchtime (see *Practice Exercises*). The arguments for reducing recess time tend to include cries for more instruction and fewer problem behaviors (e.g., aggression). Counterarguments point to studies indicating advantages of recess for children's learning and performance in class as well as for their social relations and school liking. Also, proponents of recess note that aggression on elementary playgrounds is uncommon, accounting for 2 or 3 percent of total behavior (Pellegrini, 1988), and it is often instigated by very few children (i.e., bullies). (In some schools, however, bullying is more of a problem.) Further, with appropriate supervision in positive school climates, aggressive behavior drops dramatically (e.g., Olweus Bullying Prevention Program).

So when should teachers intervene in children's peer relations? Developmental psychologists and educators often agree that attending to children's regulatory and social skills in daily classroom activities is important for developing positive relations in school. And we have just reported arguments for disengaging at times from free-play activities so that children can develop other important social skills with their peers. Vivian Paley (1992), an acclaimed kindergarten teacher and author, reported her struggles with the accepted practice to leave children alone during free-play in *You Can't Say You Can't Play*. In particular, she struggled with concerns about children who are rejected year after year, as Ladd and his colleagues documented good reasons for concern, discussed earlier. She decided to bring the question about whether to intervene to children (as she often does), and she talked with older elementary students about the fairness and effectiveness of imposing the rule, "you can't say you can't play" before she implemented it in her kindergarten classroom. Some children thought that the rule was fair, but few thought it would work because it is an intrusion into friendship. The remainder of her book revealed children's responses to the rule and delightful (and sometimes heart wrenching) conversations and stories concerning its implementation in her classroom. Paley's abilities to respect, sympathize, and communicate with both the rejectors and rejected children, and her willingness to leave them to their own devices at times, encourages children to become more accepting and accepted over time.

Fortunately, integrating practices that foster other social skills is not nearly as challenging or controversial. There are well-established programs on social skill or social and emotional learning (SEL) available to guide school and classroom practices; some have been supported by research. For example, members of CASEL have created several guides for educators. One guide outlines the curriculum scope for different age groups (Elias et al., 1997); goals for promoting children's peer relations in preschool and primary grades include the following (p. 135):

- Being a member of a group (e.g., sharing, listening, taking turns, cooperating, being considerate, helping, handling disputes)
- Initiating interactions
- Resolving conflicts without fighting (e.g., learning to compromise)
- Understanding justifiable self-defense
- Demonstrating empathy toward peers (e.g., showing emotional distress when others suffer, becoming aware of others' experiences or perspective-taking, helping rather than hurting or neglecting, supporting rather than dominating, respecting rather than belittling others)

In a more recent guide, Elias and Butler (2006) provided specific suggestions for topics and activities that can be quickly and easily integrated into the regular curriculum. Topics include effective listening, self-monitoring, assertive communication, resisting provocations, working as part of a team, conversation skills, and joining a group, among many others. Table 3.3 includes suggestions for one second-grade activity: caring for friends. Recommendations for involving parents in activities— the subject of the next section—are also provided in this guide.

Thus, to foster positive peer relations, teachers must create a balance between directing children's activities and allowing them to direct their own. This theme is expanded in Chapter 4. To reiterate specific suggestions made for promoting healthy peer relations here, teachers can (a) attend to their own interactions with children as models for their students; (b) ensure that

Table 3.3   Promoting Social Competence in the Classroom: Sample Activity for One Topic

Selecting and Caring for Friends (Second Grade)	
1.	Introduce the new topic. Ask students to close their eyes and think of their best friend.
2.	Generate a list of what makes a friend a friend. (Prompts: What kinds of things does a good friend say? What does the person do that is nice or good for a friend to do?) Then generate a list of not-good friend behaviors. (Prompts: What are some behaviors that we do not like in a friend or that makes them not fun to be around?)
3.	Conduct a practice activity. Read vignettes or scenarios involving conflicts in friendship (provided in the guide). Ask the class to generate ideas for what to do when friends act in negative ways.
4.	Construct a reflective summary. Ask students to reflect on what they have learned about friendship.
5.	Conduct follow-up activities. Praise good friendship behaviors in student interactions both inside and outside the classroom. Have students pick "Secret Friend" names, and ask students to do one thing each day that shows good friendship behaviors. Discuss experiences at the end of the week (without revealing names).

(Adapted from Elias & Butler, 2006.)

Tips for Teachers and worksheets are provided for 29 topics for each grade level (see Elias & Butler's [2006] curriculum guide listed in Resources).

all children are included in small group activities, and prompt when needed; (c) take advantage of everyday social conflicts to discuss and resolve together in class meetings (can also relate to story discussions); (d) implement child-centered, developmentally appropriate practices; (e) allow some free time in class and at recess for children to interact with minimal adult control (adults observe and monitor from a distance); (f) encourage friendships in the classroom, and allow friends to work together on academic tasks at times; (g) initiate structured games on the playground (provide materials and guidance, then let children go); (h) watch out for bullying behavior; (i) implement a social skills curriculum shown to be effective (see Resources); (j) if problems with violent behavior persist, consider implementing a proven, schoolwide SEL or prevention program (e.g., SDP, Olweus Bullying Prevention, Second Step).

TEACHER-PARENT RELATIONSHIPS AND FAMILY INVOLVEMENT IN SCHOOL

The opening window illustrated some admirable attempts by teachers to enhance their connections with parents and other family members. Teacher attitudes and efforts influence the extent to which parents and families become involved in their children's schools, and such involvement makes a big difference in children's success. Research shows that parental involvement is an indicator of children's school attendance and adjustment as well as their achievement. Parents may be involved in the education of their children at school or in the home. Attendance at school meetings, programs, and activities are the most recognizable forms of involvement. However, parents can also become involved in their children's education by providing places for educational activities, reading to them, having meaningful conversations about school, and helping children manage their time and homework. Research indicates that the extent to which parents assume these kinds of responsibilities for educating their children is important for fostering school adjustment and learning (e.g., Weiss, Caspe, & Lopez, 2006).

Joyce Epstein and her colleagues (2002) have identified six major types of family involvement and their expected impact on children, teachers, and parents (pp. 14–16):

1. *Parenting.* Help families establish home environments to support children as students. (Expected outcomes include strengthening children's attachment to school,

and their parents' confidence in parenting. Teachers also gain understanding and respect for families' strengths.)

2. *Communicating.* Design effective forms of school-to-home and home-to-school communications about school activities and children's experiences. (Expected outcomes include increasing children's understanding of their roles as students, and their parents' monitoring of their progress. Teachers also gain access to parent networks for communications.)

3. *Volunteering.* Recruit and organize parent help and support. (Expected outcomes include enhancing children's skill in communicating with adults, and parents' understanding of the teacher's job. Teachers also gain time to provide individual attention to children with volunteers in the classroom.)

4. *Learning at home.* Provide ideas about how families can help children with homework and other school-related activities. (Expected outcomes include enhancing children's attitudes toward schoolwork, and parents' awareness of their children as learners. Teachers also gain respect for family time.)

5. *Decision making.* Include parents in school decisions. (Expected outcomes include increasing children's positive experiences as a result of improved policies, and parents' feelings of ownership of school. Teachers become better aware of parent perspectives.)

6. *Collaborating with the community.* Identify and integrate community resources and services to strengthen school programs, family practices, and children's learning and development. (Expected outcomes include enhancing children's skills and talents through enriched experiences, and parents' use of needed services. Teachers become better aware of resources to enrich curriculum and services to refer families when needed.)

Sample practices are included in *School, Family, and Community Partnerships: Your Handbook for Action* (Epstein et al., 2002); see Resources.

Epstein and her colleagues (2002) noted that the type and quality of involvement matter, and they are affected by teacher-parent relations. For instance, if a teacher routinely contacts parents only when there is a behavioral or academic problem, then parents could become negative toward home-school inter-action and reduce their involvement. There are other reasons to consider why parents may be reluctant to become involved in their child's school. For example, some cultures view the teacher and the school as absolute authority and the parent's role is not to question those practices. There are often language barriers between school and home which inhibit conversation and clear understanding of expectations and goals. Also, research has indi-cated that parental educational level and socioeconomic status, as well as family size, influence the degree of parent involve-ment. Generally, those parents who are more educated and have middle incomes will be more involved than those who are poor and uneducated. Finally, research has documented the decrease of parental involvement across the grades, unless schools and teachers work to implement appropriate partnerships at each level (e.g., Rimm-Kaufman & Pianta, 2005). However, research continues to point to parental involvement being effective and needed throughout the child's entire school life. It is important to note that although we use the term "parent" here most often, we are referring to adult family members who are responsible for and provide primary care for children; these can be parents, grandparents, foster parents, older siblings, and others.

To enhance family involvement, we need to consider the motives of parents, teachers, and school personnel, and the resources or benefits they offer each other...

To enhance family involve-ment, we need to consider the motives of parents, teachers, and school personnel, and the resources or benefits they offer each other, as well as the costs of involvement (Halgunseth, 2009). For example, teachers and schools can offer welcoming environments, opportunities for interactions with other parents and community service providers, two-way communication systems, parenting classes, and educational resources for parents. In exchange, parents can provide information about their children, enhance learning experiences at home, and volunteer at school. Such healthy exchanges contribute to stronger partnerships, enhanced family engagement, and more positive child and family outcomes. We also have to consider costs of involvement; for example, requiring extensive homework can undermine quality family time just as requiring extensive teacher-family-school activities can undermine quality teacher-student time. Inappropriate expectations and demands can also undermine trust. Developing mutual trust between teachers and parents is important for commitment and engagement in productive activities, as it is in teacher-child and peer relationships.

The establishment of a reciprocal relationship with children's parents is listed as one of the core values of an excellent teacher by the NAEYC (Copple & Bredekamp, 2009). Excellent teachers see the value of involving parents not only to better understand children's strengths and weaknesses but also to understand their cultural backgrounds and family environments that influence their learning and well-being in school (including their physical health, that is, sleep, nutrition, exercise habits). They see children as part of a larger interconnected social system, which influences their social and academic competencies (see Figure 1.1), and parents as vital in this system. Therefore, excellent teachers work hard to develop mutual partnerships that function with two-way communication channels and avenues for parents to become involved in their classrooms and schools. Table 3.4 provides recommendations for teachers to initiate such partnerships. Educators might also want to join the Family Involvement Network of Educators (FINE) to learn more about promoting partnerships with children's families (see Resources).

Chapter Summary

The primacy of relationships in the early school years is becoming increasingly recognized. Relationships developed in school forecast later relationships and either support or challenge children's adjustment and learning; thus, fostering

Table 3.4 Creating Partnerships With Parents and Families

Partnership Values	Practical Suggestions
Create a warm, welcoming school and classroom atmosphere for parents to visit and participate.	• Welcome and communicate with parents using positive and relaxed body language, facial expressions, and tone of voice. • Provide a choice of activities for parents (e.g., a parent may feel more comfortable decorating bulletin boards than reading to students). • Create a parent resource room or space for parents to connect. • Address parents by name and find out some details about their lives and interests. • Spend time outside class getting to know parents (e.g., invite them to stay for lunch, come early for coffee, etc.).
Model positive communication behavior such as active listening and conflict resolution skills.	• Keep eye contact and maintain an open posture (e.g., don't cross your arms, sit behind your desk, etc.) when talking. • Listen with the intention of "checking in" to make sure parents' concerns are heard (e.g., "I can see that you are worried about your child's progress and stress level. Can you tell me more about why you are concerned?"). • Use language translators whenever there is a language barrier or when parents feel more comfortable communicating in their native language.
Commit to ongoing two-way communication channels that become part of the school and classroom culture.	• Distribute routine notes, memos, or photos about classroom news. • Provide a central place in the classroom where parents can go for more information. • Use the Internet, e-mail, and homework webpage to communicate ideas, events, quotes for the week, and so forth. • Incorporate home visits, especially for transitions to elementary school. • Use parent surveys to solicit input on various classroom practices, and identify their talents, skills, and availability.

Provide avenues of respect and sensitivity for parents to express their goals, choices, and concerns about their children.	• Value and model these beliefs. • Reflect (write about) your feelings about parents and potential conflicts. • Seek out a trusted mentor educator to discuss feelings and ideas.

positive relationships is central in successful school reform efforts. We began with a look at the quality of teacher-student relationships, how these relationships might be formed and perpetuated, and how to enhance positive relationships, even with children who challenge teacher efforts. We also discussed the importance of peer relationships in school and what teachers can do to promote (and refrain from inhibiting) these relationships in and out of the classroom. Finally, we looked at research demonstrating the value of creating partnerships with children's parents and families to further children's development and learning in school. A theme of this chapter is that children, parents, and teachers need regular opportunities for positive interactions to build relationships and the support of others to perform well in their roles.

Questions to Ponder

1. Think of individual children in preschool or the primary grades with whom you have enjoyed both positive and less positive relationships, and respond to the questions listed in Table 3.1. Considering the material in this chapter, attempt to explain the reasons for the quality of these relationships from the children's perspectives.

2. Think about Katie in *The Child's Window*. Considering the brief background provided, what do you think explains her current problems with the teacher and peers? What would you do at the parent conference

if you were in Mrs. Snow's shoes? How would you change things in the classroom? Refer to information from this chapter to form your responses.

3. As a prospective or practicing teacher, what are your attitudes toward "partnering" with parents? (See Table 3.4.)

Practice Exercises

1. **Relations in the Classroom.** Ask a preschooler or primary-grade child about his or her relationships in class using the items in Table 3.2. You can use a rating scale similar to the one described in the Practice Exercises in Chapter 2. Ask the child to explain his or her ratings. What other questions or items might you add to find out more about the child's relationships with classmates?

2. **How Was Your Day at School?** Ask a preschool or primary-grade child to "tell me about your day at school." What was the child's first response? You can probe a bit by asking, "What did you do in class, on the playground, at lunch," and so forth, to elicit more details. Note the mention of relationship themes.

3. **Parents as Partners.** Choose one or two of the partnership values and consider how you might express these as a teacher. What difficulties would you expect? What outcomes would you value?

Key Words

Attachment theory

Working models

Conflicted relationships

Dependent relationships

Close relationships

Social competence

4

Developmentally Appropriate Classroom Practices

Fostering Learning in the Classroom

Window Into Practice

Krystal Smith had always wanted to be a teacher. Even from a young age, she envisioned what her classroom would look like—where she would set up the reading corner, which animals she would have for children to care for, and how she would take the time to get to know each child. Upon completing her teaching credential, Krystal accepted a teaching position for a third-grade class in a poor school district near her home. This district served a large population of Native Americans as well as Latino/a and White families. Many families were from low income groups. The school principal valued teacher-to-teacher communication, peer coaching between teachers, and facilitated discussions about transition between grades. Krystal met with her students' previous teachers to discuss academic assessments, behavior plans and modifications, and strategies that had been successful and unsuccessful with individuals the past year. Krystal felt that this type of collaboration was invaluable to her as an educator and she was grateful for the support and information that was shared.

Krystal gained access to her classroom weeks before orientation, just so she could set up her room and begin planning. She took great care to create a physical environment which would appeal to third graders. Everything in her room was child height and the different reading corners were her pride and joy. Krystal had scoured garage sales and used bookstores to find just the right "classics" that would surely capture her young readers' interest and ignite a love for reading. She had soft couches and fun, comfortable chairs to create a warm atmosphere to explore books. Krystal arranged the desks in "table groups," which had their own tub of community supplies to be shared by the table (i.e., glue, crayons, markers, scissors). The children would have their own pencils and erasers, but the remaining supplies would be shared using the table "tub." Krystal felt strongly that the class needed to learn how to function as a community and take care of each other and the classroom they shared. Next, Krystal created name tags for each child and files that would hold valuable, personal reflections as she observed and assessed their growth.

When the first day of school finally arrived, Krystal could hardly ignore her pounding heart as she greeted students at the door, handing them their name tags and instructing them to hang up their backpacks and find seats on the carpet. Throughout the next few weeks, Krystal learned to adapt her teaching practices and classroom management style to her students. She and the children created simple signals, such as a finger on their nose, when they were to become quiet for instructions. The children created a simple set of classroom rules such as, "no name calling" and "talk to your neighbor about the problem." The children were rotated through a series of classroom "jobs" as well. Everyone participated in keeping the classroom running efficiently. Student jobs consisted of filing, taking attendance, recycling, caring for class pets and plants, and cleaning (the sanitation crew). These tasks contributed to the classroom "community," which Krystal felt was important for children's growth and development of a sense of responsibility for their classroom.

Krystal also met each of her student's parents long before parent conferences either in person, by phone, by e-mail, or through notes. As the school year progressed, she was careful to convey positive information to parents as well as ask for assistance with more difficult behaviors.

Krystal's greatest challenge was interacting with Alex. Alex had been placed in her classroom because he needed extra care, extra help, and lots of patience. Alex had been diagnosed with attention deficit/hyperactivity disorder, obsessive/compulsive disorder, and other sensory disorders, which resulted in a 504 Health Impairment Plan. He was not assigned an instructional aide. Alex only left the classroom for 10 minutes each day to work with a specialist on literacy skills, so for the vast majority of his day, he was in Krystal's third-grade class. Krystal was determined to include Alex in every activity and learning opportunity. She wanted to show him that he could excel beyond his expectations, and she wanted the rest of her third graders to experience and adapt to differences in other people. Krystal felt that this was a life experience that most of these children needed, and she enjoyed working beside them to model respect, kindness, care, and selflessness. On a daily basis, Alex drew attention to himself by singing loudly, talking out of turn, and tapping his pencil uncontrollably. Krystal would respond by capturing Alex's attention eye-to-eye and then engaging him in a brief conversation about the particular behavior that needed correction. The rest of the third graders learned to communicate with Alex in the same manner. Through Krystal's modeling and guidance, Alex's classmates began to express their feelings and give Alex the opportunity to respond, rather than yell at him to stop or constantly tattle to Krystal to fix the problem. The classroom climate beamed with student-to-student support, collaboration, and constructive debates. The children figured out how to solve conflicts respectfully and how to seek solutions of compromise. By having Alex part of the classroom, the rest of the children learned how to practice empathy and community and how to take responsibility for their own actions. Alex learned that the social world he lived in wasn't always so patient and that he had a responsibility to put forth his best effort to listen and respond to the requests of his peers. Alex also began to realize that he couldn't use his disability as an excuse to cause disruption when things got tough for him. Instead, he began to feel empowered to want to change those behaviors that caused the classroom to become disrupted.

By the end of the year, Krystal had adapted her instructional practices to mold to her students. She passed on a group of new fourth graders who took pride in their classroom community and who possessed the skills to resolve conflicts respectfully and demonstrate empathy for others. Krystal was proud of their academic accomplishments, and she beamed while recounting stories of mutual respect, trust, and collaborative efforts that appeared beyond average behavior for the typical third grader.

Krystal's experience illustrates a teacher adapting her practices to fit children's developmental needs and skills. She was determined from the beginning to make a difference for this class of children, and she succeeded in keeping a balance of child-directed and **teacher-directed** classroom practices. The adaptation process that Krystal experienced her first year has its roots in contemporary **developmentally appropriate** or **learner-centered** approaches to education (also referred to as **child-centered**). The NAEYC is a leader in providing current guiding principles for teaching children through age 8 supported by sound research. NAEYC's guidelines for developmentally appropriate practice stem from beliefs that both *child-directed* and *teacher-directed* practices are necessary for children's optimal learning and development. A successful teacher can apply clear expectations, explanations, and directions while allowing children hands-on experiences and opportunities for decision making (Copple & Bredekamp, 2009). The figure shows the "balance" that is necessary for teachers to adapt practices to fit the developmental needs of children in their classrooms (see Figure 4.1).

Figure 4.1   Balancing Child-Directed And Teacher-Directed Approaches

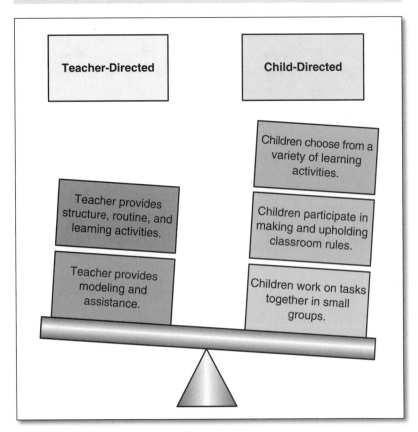

The chapter begins with an introduction to basic ideas about how children develop intellectually from **constructivist perspectives**. These theoretical explanations provide the founda-

At the heart of constructivist perspectives is a focus on the mind of the child or learner.

tion for many contemporary approaches to education advocated today. At the heart of constructivist perspectives is a focus on the mind of the child or learner. Thus, the terms child-, learner-, or student-*centered* are often used to describe constructivist practices. Constructivist, child-centered practices are considered "developmentally appropriate" because they begin with attending to the development of the child; thus, they are advocated by educational psychologists and organizations like NAEYC, as noted throughout this book. Oftentimes, child-centered practices are contrasted with *teacher*-centered practices ("traditional"). These practices are based on beliefs that teachers mold children's learning primarily through direct instruction and rewards and reinforcement; the teacher is the center of attention rather than how children interpret experiences or construct their own learning. (Note that teacher-*centered* practices are different from teacher-*directed* practices, which are used in conjunction with child-directed practices in constructivist classrooms.)

After introducing theoretical approaches and briefly highlighting the importance of play in development, we attend to three major components of quality educational practices: (a) classroom climate, (b) classroom organization, and (c) classroom instruction. We make a few general recommendations for practice here to add to those provided in previous chapters (they cannot "stand alone"). Readers are encouraged to look to other books in the *Classroom Insights* series for specific instructional practices and guidance in teaching particular subject areas (e.g., science).

SOCIAL-CONSTRUCTIVIST APPROACHES

Approaches that attempt to balance child- and teacher-directed learning activities stem primarily from a **social-constructivist** theoretical perspective. Lev Vygotsky, a noted Russian psychologist, proposed a sociocultural theory of children's development and learning. According to Vygotsky (1978), learning is socially based and children master meaningful cultural activities (i.e., literacy) through guided participation by adults and more sophisticated peers (e.g., Bodrova & Leong, 2007; Rogoff, Turkanis, & Bartlett, 2001; Wilkinson & Silliman, 1997). Within the "**zone of proximal development**" (ZPD), an adult or competent peer intentionally supports development within the scope of tasks children cannot achieve by themselves but would be able to accomplish with assistance. Based on Vygotsky's conception, Bodrova and Leong (2007) referred to the "zone" as the area of development between a child's present point of skill and those skills that the child would be able to develop in the near future. Children need less assistance as they develop competencies in one area and more as they encounter new areas or tasks. Constructivists believe that children play an active role in acquiring knowledge rather than a passive "waiting to be filled" role.

Many teachers have integrated social constructivist practices into their instructional approaches. For example, **scaffolding** is a common strategy introduced in teacher preparation programs. Teachers "scaffold" children's learning beyond what they can accomplish on their own to what is currently just out of reach by providing models, hints, and cues as well as other means of assistance. However, there is a level of accomplishment beyond a child's current ZPD in which the child will not be able to benefit from instruction. For example, a 5-year-old beginning to learn to write the letters in her name would not be ready to write a sentence or a paragraph even with appropriate instruction. Teachers also use *instructional conversations* by listening carefully to children, making assumptions about their meaning, and adjusting their responses to help children develop more sophisticated understandings of concepts (e.g., Tharp & Gallimore, 1988). These conversations often occur in small groups.

Social-cultural researchers, such as Roland Tharp, Ron Gallimore, and William Doherty, have incorporated these ideas and processes into standards for effective teaching practices. The *Five Standards* were derived from many years of research with children of all ages, particularly those at risk for academic failure due to poverty or cultural or language barriers (e.g., Center for Research on Education, Diversity & Excellence, 2010; Doherty & Hilberg, 2007). The Five Standards can be summarized as follows:

1. Learning is facilitated when teachers and students work together in joint productive activity.

2. Students must develop competence in the language and literacy of instruction.

3. Curriculum must be meaningful, based on previous knowledge, and connected to students' lives (e.g., home, community).

4. Learning activities must be challenging, requiring complex thinking.

5. Teachers need to engage children through dialogue, especially instructional conversations.

These standards are consistent with recommendations made by other constructivist educators, and they are often included in assessments of classroom quality; instructional practices such as these are discussed later in the chapter.

Educators have also relied on another prominent child development theorist, Jean Piaget, to help understand and support children's development and learning. Piaget (1926, 1960) asserted that children create their own knowledge through interactions with their environment and others; his views and descriptions of thinking in childhood have provided the impetus for constructivist educational practices or child-centered approaches (Elkind, 1976; Sigel, 1978). Children construct input from the environment through assimilating and accommodating information into their own mental models, thereby deepening their understanding as they gain experience. Piaget also emphasized the importance of children's *active* engagement with materials and others and their learning through play.

Engagement in variations of play (physical, social, pretend, and constructive) has been associated with advances in memory, language abilities, social skills, self-regulation, and success in school (see recent reviews in Elkind, 2009; Hirsch-Pasek, Golinkoff, Berk, & Singer, 2009). The different types of play include the following:

- *Physical Play (with or without rules):* Running, jumping, swinging, and sliding are typical physical play activities not accompanied by rules, and they provide obvious physical and psychological benefits to children. Physical play with rules such as soccer, basketball, or hide-and-seek are useful in promoting associations with "laws," which children must learn to follow to live productively.
- *Social Play:* Through all forms of play with others, children learn how to interact in a prosocial manner. Cooperation, sharing, and compromise are present in social play where moral reasoning develops. These interactions prepare children for collaborating and learning with peers and others.
- *Pretend Play:* This type of play allows children to experiment with new roles and scenarios in a safe environment. They "try on" new identities, experimenting with language and different feelings. Children learn to be flexible thinkers and their imagination is stretched, as scenarios take on different directions. Engagement in this type of play is linked to advances in literacy skills.
- *Constructive Play:* This type of play allows children to create things as they interact with their environment. For example, children build cities, castles, and towers with blocks, and they create masterful artwork with chalk on a sidewalk. Constructive play allows children to try out what works and what doesn't work while adding to their basic knowledge, for example, in areas of building, stacking, and drawing. Engagement in this type of play is linked to advances in math and science learning.

Excellent teachers have implemented play into their daily classroom routines to foster children's learning and development.

Developmental and educational psychologists and organizations such as NAEYC provide frameworks based on constructivist and social-constructivist theories for guiding developmentally appropriate practices. Guidelines for creating quality classroom climates, organizational practices, and instructional supports for children in preschool and the primary grades are included. Researchers have developed measures to assess quality practices in each of these three related classroom domains: (a) climate, (b) organization, and (c) instruction. Each of these domains of classroom practices is discussed in more detail later. Major measures of preschool and primary-grade classroom quality include the Classroom Assessment Scoring System (CLASS), developed by Pianta and his colleagues (see, e.g., Hamre & Pianta, 2007); the Early Childhood Classroom Observation Measure (ECCOM; Stipek & Byler, 2004); and the Early Childhood Environmental Rating Scale-Revised (ECERS-R; Harms, Clifford, & Cryer, 1998). These measures provide specific descriptions of quality practices linked to positive child outcomes. For example, children demonstrate more positive approaches to learning in constructivist classrooms than in traditional, didactic classrooms (see, e.g., Stipek & Byler, 2004). Some descriptions of quality practices from these measures are incorporated in the tables in this chapter as examples; teachers can refer to these to analyze the quality of their own classroom practices.

Classroom Climate

Classroom climate refers to the social/emotional atmosphere of the classroom. Pianta and his colleagues described the emotional climate as the amount of enthusiasm and emotional connection displayed between teachers and their students (Pianta, La Paro, & Hamre, 2008). Research has

> Emotionally supportive classrooms have been associated with lower levels of internalizing behavior (i.e., anxiety) and higher competence in children.

supported the importance of the classroom climate. As discussed in Chapter 3, it is imperative that children have a sense of security, respect, and positive relationships with their teacher and their peers in the classroom (e.g., McCombs & Miller, 2007). A quality classroom climate also includes an atmosphere where children are not afraid to make mistakes and enjoy an environment that is physically and emotionally safe. Emotionally supportive classrooms have been associated with lower levels of internalizing behavior (i.e., anxiety) and higher competence in children (NICHD ECCRN, 2003). Furthermore, teacher sensitivity has been shown to positively affect student engagement and self-reliance as well as academic outcomes, such as stronger vocabulary and decoding skills in preschoolers (Pianta et al., 2007). *Sensitivity* can be defined as the awareness of children's needs and responsiveness to address needs in all areas (physical, emotional, social, cognitive). Thus, classroom climate plays an important role in academic success, self-regulation development, and intellectual competence, and it should be regarded as an essential area of classroom quality evaluation.

The physical arrangement of the desks, the décor, and inclusion of items in the classroom such as pets, gardens, and relaxing reading corners contribute to the atmosphere of the classroom. Children and teachers need an interesting physical environment where they feel comfortable, relaxed, and secure to establish relationships and learn. Best teaching practices also include cultivating a caring community within the classroom and taking the responsibility to know each child individually as well as establishing a routine schedule. For example, in the opening *Window,* Krystal carefully planned the physical arrangement of her room to include table groups to facilitate "community" and comfortable "home-like" spaces for relaxed reading. She also cultivated a community in her classroom by assigning classroom "jobs" on a rotating basis. The children were able to share in the workload and feel a sense of ownership of their classroom. Several resources are available to help educators create a community of learners.

In addition, teachers can model appropriate caring behaviors. For example, Krystal, in the opening *Window,* treated Alex with kindness and provided simple explanations for what she wanted him to do and why, while the other children in the classroom observed. When Alex posed challenges, children mimicked her behavior and supported each other's efforts to help him. Krystal also used specific praise in reinforcing positive behaviors in all the children. For example, she often commented on their cooperation. Alex and the other children noticed the praise and made sure their behavior was noteworthy. (Specific recommendations for providing feedback are included in *Resource C, Guides for Practice;* see also Good & Brophy, 2007; Stipek, 2002b.) Building from secure relationships, Krystal's students were able to establish trust with Alex and model positive interactions. In turn, Alex started to experience the social benefits and improve his behavior.

Table 4.1 provides a list of easily observable teacher and classroom qualities that reflect a positive classroom climate.

Table 4.1   Classroom Climate: Teacher and Classroom Qualities

Teacher Qualities	Examples
Enthusiasm	Uses facial expressions to show happiness and tone of voice to communicate excitement about classroom activities.
Enjoyment	Smiles often and regards challenges as opportunities to grow.
Connection	Makes eye contact with children and responds to comments and questions in a pleasant tone.
Responsiveness	Invites children to ask questions and validates opinions with a response (verbally and nonverbally).
Security	Demonstrates fairness and respect for each individual child (consistency). Does not show favoritism. Keeps in confidence the feelings and personal comments made by children.

(Continued)

(Continued)

Classroom Qualities	Examples
Variety and Choice	• Many "interest" centers organized around recent learning themes • Soft, cozy places for reading or quiet activities • Spaces for group work and collaboration (i.e., desks arranged in groups) • Manipulatives accessible and labeled for use • Child-directed, "hands-on" (sensory) learning materials available • Photographs and recent work from the children displayed around the classroom
Movement	• Ample space for movement and accessible to disabled children • Furnishings in good repair and free from causing injury or inhibiting movement • Room to walk between learning areas
Physical Space	• Child-sized furnishings and décor • Lots of natural light in the classroom • Good ventilation • Clean and organized spaces • Well-maintained equipment and furnishings

CLASSROOM ORGANIZATION

Classroom organization practices consist of many activities, including routines, behavioral strategies, and "housekeeping" tasks. These classroom processes have been the focus of researchers for years. Hamre and Pianta (2007) divided classroom organization into three broad categories:

- *Productivity.* Refers to the classroom routines and organization as well as student engagement.
- *Behavior management.* Refers to the ways in which teachers effectively manage and promote positive behavior in the classroom.

- *Instructional formats.* Refers to the activities and learning objectives in the classroom and student choices in those objectives.

The formation of these practice areas was influenced by the work of many developmental and educational psychologists, highlighting successful processes that promote children's engagement in the learning process, such as provision of meaningful activities and guidance toward more challenging work (see previous *Five Standards*). Practices in these three areas often relate to one another. In Chapter 2, we noted that high quality organizational practices foster children's self-regulation, among other skills critical for school adjustment and achievement.

Children's engagement in *productive*, interesting activities is a central theme for successful classroom flow and organization, as well as for prevention of mis-

Children's engagement in *productive*, interesting activities is a central theme for successful classroom flow and organization, as well as for prevention of misbehavior.

behavior. Historically, research has supported the premise that children who are bored or left with "nothing to do" will begin to engage in negative and disruptive behaviors that take away from classroom learning and demand precious attention from the teacher (Brophy & Good, 1986). Furthermore, teachers can curtail misbehavior when they implement a few key practices into an efficient classroom routine. Current research also suggests that teachers can be productive by planning worthwhile lessons and individual follow-up activities and working with individual and small groups of children. For example, giving children interesting activity choices when they are finished with their work, assuring that assignments and lessons are challenging and meaningful, and continuously moving around the classroom to provide feedback and attention are ways teachers can keep children engaged. Successful classroom organizers rarely sit alone at teacher desks during class time.

Talking to children about expected behavior and then "living it out" in the classroom speaks volumes to children, and they will gain a sense of the classroom "culture" and practices which in turn will aid in *managing classroom behavior.* Children's development at school starts with a nurturing relationship with the teacher (see Chapter 3) and learning how to better manage their behavior and collaborate with others (see Chapter 2). Teachers foster collaboration in the early primary grades by providing opportunities for children to work together on learning projects, molding lessons to allow individuals to contribute, and integrating role-playing situations. These practices also minimize negative behavior. In the *Window Into Practice* vignette at the beginning of this chapter, Krystal demonstrated positive strategies by helping her children take initiative to solve their conflicts through role-playing and collaborative input into the "rules" of the classroom. These strategies helped shape the culture of her classroom and provided the foundation for a community of learners to evolve. The shaping of a community of learners is also beautifully illustrated in the book by Barbara Rogoff and her colleagues (2001), *Learning Together: Children and Adults in a School Community* (see Resource C).

Research on constructivist early education also supports providing children opportunities to make meaningful choices (e.g., Stipek et al., 1998). When children are given choices within the perimeters of the classroom structure, they are able to assert some independence and initiative, which promotes their development and success in school (see Chapter 2). For example, Krystal provided many choices after work was completed and checked. Children were able to choose a quiet reading corner, a listening activity, or art center for follow-up learning activities. According to Rogoff et al. (2001), children feel a sense of ownership and enthusiasm when they are able to choose the time and sequence in finishing certain activities. Consequently, children who are engaged in their own active learning see disruptive behavior as a nuisance and a waste of time, much like how classmates took it upon themselves to problem-solve with Alex to reduce his distracting behavior so they could continue their activities (see *Windows*).

Effective *instructional formats* involve making use of instructional time to maximize children's active participation and learning opportunities. For example, in the well-examined

KEEP program, teachers spent much of their time working together with children in small groups on thoughtfully planned literacy lessons, often engaging in instructional conversations (Tharp & Gallimore, 1988). Other children were engaged in supportive learning activities and assisted one another. These practices are consistent with the *Five Standards* established later on the basis of studying this successful program and others.

Effective instructional formats also allow teachers to delve into their extensive "tool boxes" and choose appropriate tools to facilitate children's learning and development (Copple & Bredekamp, 2009). For example, a teacher might anticipate a lesson on the life cycle of a butterfly to be interesting and engaging for her class. Upon seeing the larva, the children immediately express a fascination with the tiny embryo. The teacher could change the direction of the lesson (her tool) in order to capitalize on the enthusiasm and interest of the children. The children might spend more time discussing and exploring the attributes of the larva, making connections to other creatures with similar characteristics, and possibly not complete the lesson on the butterfly life cycle that day. Children are engaged in learning activities with materials and interactions with others in a positive, somewhat flexible, classroom organization.

Playful learning is an example of an instructional format essential for optimal learning in childhood (e.g., Hirsch-Pasek et al., 2009). Playful learning is enjoyable guided play that appears spontaneous and encourages academic exploration and learning. It is connected to learning goals set by educators and designed to build on children's previous knowledge and experiences. As noted earlier, providing a classroom that supports learning through play (physical, social, pretend, and constructive) will facilitate children's growth in memory, language, social skills, self-regulation, and school success. *Tools of the Mind* is an example of an educational program that incorporates playful learning in systematic ways to build children's self-regulation and complex thinking skills (see Chapter 2 and Resources).

Table 4.2 provides descriptions of sample practices representing high quality, constructivist classroom organizational practices.

Table 4.2   Classroom Organization

	Examples
Productivity	• Children work in small groups with specific tasks to accomplish. • The teacher moves around the classroom providing feedback and attention to keep children engaged. • The teacher encourages peer conversations about the stories at the reading center. • Children have a sense of ownership of the classroom rules and feel a sense of responsibility to uphold those rules. • Children are engaged in "jobs" which support classroom routines.
Behavior Management	• Children participate in creating classroom rules (i.e., "no talking bad about classmates"). • The teacher uses role-playing to foster interpersonal skills and manage conflict. • The teacher uses both positive and negative consequences depending on the behavior. The tone is calm and nonthreatening. • The teacher models expected behavior such as "inside tone" of voice, manners, and listening to students. • Children work individually or in small groups with plenty of follow-up activities to choose from when they are finished.
Instructional Format	• The teacher provides challenging and meaningful assignments and lessons. • The teacher responds to children's interest in a particular topic and expands the activity to include time to explore their interests. • Children are able to choose materials they prefer to complete a project. • The teacher provides a variety of reading levels while encouraging students to choose books just beyond their current skill level. • The teacher provides time to engage in meaningful play opportunities.

CLASSROOM INSTRUCTION

The third major domain of classroom practice is **instructional support.** Based on social constructivist perspectives, quality classrooms have scaffolded practices embedded into the instruction. Teachers provide a "roadmap" of learning outcomes to help guide children along the path (Bodrova & Leong, 2007). Instruction in the classroom then assists each child while traveling down the road. For example, to assist children in learning to classify animals, a teacher might provide areas identified as potential homes for the animals (i.e., water, desert, forest). Then, children can place each animal where they feel it would live. Once children have placed each animal in a home, the teacher can engage them in a lively discussion (instructional conversation) about the attributes of each home and why each particular animal needs that home to survive. Quality instruction challenges children to stretch just beyond their current skill level and gives ample opportunities for children to practice their newly acquired skills.

A sample instructional strategy is **reciprocal teaching**. Reciprocal teaching is an excellent example of applying Vygotsky's social-cultural theory in the classroom (Brown, 1997; Brown & Campione, 1990). Reciprocal teaching is a group discussion between students and the teacher (or adult) designed to strengthen reading comprehension skills. The teacher may ask questions about a story requiring children to summarize, infer, make predictions, or explain inconsistencies. As the children gain mastery synthesizing the story, the teacher increases the level of challenging questions. Eventually, children become the leaders of the discussion and the teacher reduces his role to a coach or mentor. Reciprocal teaching allows the less competent student to step up to more difficult levels as the teacher carefully scaffolds. It also supports analysis and reasoning skills as children are reaffirmed and encouraged to explore the elements of the story. Research on the use of reciprocal teaching has shown great improvements in student comprehension, even in a short amount of time. In addition, reciprocal teaching supports a better understanding of science and social studies curriculum content.

... quality teachers consistently ask open-ended questions and expand children's responses. They are clearly intentional about their instructional efforts. ...

Reciprocal teaching has also been shown to support at-risk readers as well. For example, Brown (1997) reported that participants in reciprocal teaching groups improved their comprehension and they maintained their advantage even after 1 year.

Quality instructional support also involves *intentional language stimulation* and facilitation. Teachers display a variety of self-talk, parallel-talk, open-ended questions, and repetitive language while providing positive feedback and focus on the learning process, not just outcomes. Research suggests that in classrooms where such instructional supports are used, such as feedback and language modeling, children show achievement gains (e.g., Pianta et al., 2007). These gains are evident in literacy skills (reading, vocabulary, language), as well as social adjustment. Research also shows that quality teachers consistently ask open-ended questions and expand children's responses. They are clearly intentional about their instructional efforts and they support peer conversations.

Classroom instructional practices are most effective when they contain a *wide variety of activities and interactions.* NAEYC supports instructional practices incorporating close monitoring of individual children's progress and planning purposeful learning experiences based on understandings of curricular goals (Copple & Bredekamp, 2009). Krystal, in the opening *Window,* took time before the school year started to collaborate with prior teachers and discuss her new students, gaining valuable information about them personally, socially, and academically. With this information, she was able to plan instructional lessons that were flexible and tailored to the children's interests and challenges. In order to guide instruction with intention and purpose, quality teachers recognize children's interests and involvement in the planning process.

Regardless of the curriculum standards, individual teachers can create supportive practices to facilitate academic learning. In addition to aspects of effective instruction discussed so far, key elements of quality instructional practices in classrooms include the following:

- Attending to individual skill levels and making adjustments as needed
- Providing an extension of lessons for children who are ready to move ahead
- Basing lessons on children's prior knowledge
- Rotating learning centers, materials, and books to keep children interested and curious
- Keeping lessons and activities relevant to a child's world

Summary of the Three Domains of Classroom Practice

Balancing child- and teacher-directed classroom practices takes time, reflection, and practice. As teachers focus on classroom climate, organization, and instruction, they can begin the process of seeing the environment through the children's eyes. If teachers are to embrace constructivist practices in their classroom, then their attention must be centered on the mind and heart of the child. Consistent monitoring of feedback from children is essential to understanding if effective learning is taking place. Table 4.3 includes questions teachers might ask themselves to check their instructional intentions and flexibility in a constructivist classroom. Many of these questions require feedback from the children themselves.

Quality instructional supports, classroom organization, and positive classroom climates make great differences in children's learning and achievement. As Alex recalls his experience in his third-grade classroom, described in *The Child's Window*, high quality practices in these three domains were

Table 4.3   Child-Centered Thinking

How many children are interested in this current activity?
Which children need another avenue for learning this activity?
How will I choose that alternative avenue for those children?
Is there a new skill that the children are learning with the activity?
What other impacts on learning might this activity have?
How can I relate this activity to the children's lives and make it relevant?
Is there a change in our classroom schedule that needs adjustment to accommodate this learning?
If so, how might this change in schedule impact the rest of the school day?
How might I engage those children that seem to have difficulty with this activity?

(Adapted from Rogoff et al., 2001, p. 100.)

evident and instrumental in shaping him to become a successful learner and high school graduate.

The Child's Window

Alex looked out over the audience of parents, family, friends, and teachers. It was high school graduation day and he could hardly believe his formal school years were completed. He remembered his elementary days and couldn't help but smile when he thought of Mrs. Smith's third-grade class. He remembered how he felt the first few weeks of class. He was nervous and confused. Alex remembered Mrs. Smith's warm smile and the way she would look into his eyes as if to say that everything would be ok. He remembered his friends, Kevin, Alyssa, and Clint. He remembered how they would take the time to explain things to him when he forgot the instructions. He remembered how good he felt when he shared the crayons and glue sticks with his tablemates. Alex even smiled when he thought of all the weekly "jobs" he and his classmates participated in to keep their classroom clean and organized. He remembered Mrs. Smith telling them that it was their classroom and it was their responsibility to maintain it so they would be ready to learn. By participating in responsibilities as a "table team," Alex began to understand the power of this classroom process. Although he didn't realize it at the time, Alex felt accepted in his third-grade class. It wasn't perfect; there were many instances of conflict, arguing, and tears. But, through it all, Alex remembered feeling accepted in school for the first time. After that year, he didn't feel lonely or rejected anymore. He understood how to treat people with respect and how to accept differences in others. He also had developed confidence in his academic abilities. Alex could recall how Mrs. Smith used familiar concepts such as drawing circles to help him understand how to write cursive letters. Now, on graduation day, Alex recognized that he understood these things because Mrs. Smith created an accepting environment in his third-grade classroom. Alex felt happy and confident that he could live his life like Mrs. Smith did. Alex was determined to make a difference for others in just that same way!

CHAPTER SUMMARY

Quality classroom practices continue to be a source of discussion and analysis in the fields of education and psychology. Social constructivist theories point to the use of scaffolded instruction and sensitivity to learners' ZPD; the teacher becomes a guide and participant in the learning process. These developmentally appropriate, learner-centered practices have positive influences on children's motivation, self-regulation, and academic achievement, and therefore, they are central to our understanding of successful teachers. NAEYC and other professional organizations have provided guiding principles for developmentally appropriate practices, which reflect sound research and a strong theoretical base (see Resources). The ECCOM, ECERS-R, and CLASS are effective measures monitoring the quality of classroom climate, organization, and instructional support. These three related domains of classroom practice are critical to evaluate and modify with intention and purpose as we continue to improve education in the early years and beyond.

Questions to Ponder

1. Reflect on the *Window Into Practice* story at the beginning of the chapter. What types of climate qualities do you see incorporated into the classroom before the school year even begins? How might you incorporate some of these qualities into a classroom climate?

2. Ask yourself the "child-centered thinking" questions in Table 4.3. How can you change a lesson or activity to be more child-centered?

Practice Exercises

1. **Classroom Climate.** Refer to Table 4.1. What do you think children would say about the climate of a classroom?

2. **Classroom Organization.** Examine the organization of a classroom. Do you see evidence of constructivist practices? Refer to Table 4.2.

3. **Instructional Support.** Create a sample lesson for preschoolers or primary-grade children. Rate your lesson from 1 to 5 (1 = *not at all*, 5 = *very*) on the following items:

   - Have I based my lesson on children's prior knowledge?
   - Have I provided "hands-on," real experiences whenever possible?
   - Did I attend to individual children's skill levels, making adjustments as needed?
   - Did I provide an extension of my lesson for children who might be ready to move ahead?

How could you improve your responses to these questions?

Key Words

Developmentally appropriate practices (DAP)

Learner (child)-centered practices

Teacher-directed

Social-constructivist learning theory

Zone of proximal development

Scaffolding

Classroom climate

Classroom organization

Playful learning

Classroom instructional support

Reciprocal teaching

5

Children's Learning in Digital and Natural Environments

Connecting Learning Out of the Classroom

Window Into Practice

Robert Flores was delighted to receive a generous grant to purchase new technology for his third-grade class. His students had been working with an overhead projector and paper-and-pencil methods for the past 5 years and he felt that they were ill-equipped to communicate and retrieve information in the 21st century. Most of his students came from low socioeconomic backgrounds and few had computers with current software in their homes. The elementary school had provided a computer lab for the lower grades, but the 1-hour per week computer class didn't seem to be enough. The children were learning far more about advanced technology from their more affluent classmates using cell phones, iPods, and notebook computers. Robert wanted to be able to put day-to-day technology in the hands of his students and show them the possibilities for learning about the world.

The first purchase Robert made was a handheld computer for every student. He owned one himself and felt that it provided a variety of educational avenues. Next, he purchased a small video camera and a handheld video projector for students to display and share information with each other as well as larger audiences. Next, it was time to educate children about the use of the equipment. To his surprise, most of the children had the basic operational knowledge of the technology; however, their primary use seemed to center around finding music videos and the latest computer games. Robert showed children how to search for basic information, to locate maps, and to record observational findings.

After a few weeks of training, the children were ready to venture out of the classroom and put their new technology to work. It was fall and time for the annual trip to the local apple farm. The apple farm provided a wealth of opportunities for the students to gather information and report back to the class. Robert divided the class into different "teams" of investigators. One team was to interview the apple farm owner, one team was in charge of learning about the geographic location and layout of the farm, another team was to investigate the other produce at the farm, and one team was to report on how this farm compared to other apple farms in the state. Robert challenged children to make full use of the technology in their hands; this included searching assigned websites on the Internet for facts and graphics, recording observations either by voice or type, taking relevant pictures and videos to capture their experiences, and sharing information with their classmates across the Internet while they were "in the field."

When the children returned to the classroom, Robert could hardly quiet their enthusiasm to give them the next instructions. Children were viewing each other's findings on their computers and discussing the facts and their revelations. After Robert led a class discussion to debrief the day and resolve concerns, they began collaborating to share their information on the "big screen." This process took 2 weeks to complete, but it was well worth the wait. Robert held back his tears when the class presented their "Investigation of an Apple Farm" project. Robert admired the in-depth reporting and attention to details as the children told the story of the apple farm; the maps, graphs, and comparison charts were relevant and informative. But the greatest impact of this project came from the motivation of his students. They were able to unlock a world of learning and share it, working together. Robert understood that obtaining the technology grant was not just about learning how to operate a handheld computer; it was about allowing children access to the world, to the enjoyment of learning, and to the excitement of sharing that knowledge with others!

This *Window* depicts a teacher using technology in the classroom under the best of circumstances. He has created a learning activity that is developmentally appropriate for third grade (NAEYC, 1996) and helps children become technically literate (International Society for Technology in Education, 2007) while learning a host of academic and collaborative skills. In addition, this activity was especially meaningful and engaging because it was connected to real-world experiences in the local community. It also helped to reduce the **digital divide,** or the unequal access to computer technologies among children from different income groups (Woodard & Gridina, 2000). Of course, not all teachers can provide their students with personal portable computers, but they can and do find creative ways to use technology to connect learning to life outside the classroom. David Elkind (2009), a prominent developmental psychologist, claimed that our new technologies are allowing children to revisit the project method inspired by John Dewey in "fresh and novel ways" (p. 196). He suggested that children learn best when they are challenged by these types of project-based learning activities that combine creativity, motivation, and practical and academic skills. Other constructivist theorists and educators agree that computers are powerful tools for designing and supporting meaningful learning experiences for young children (e.g., Wang & Hoot, 2006).

This chapter begins with a brief introduction to the influences of technology on the learning and development of preschool and primary-grade children. Although some attention is given to concerns about children's uses of electronic media, the focus here is on active and developmentally appropriate uses of technology for educational purposes. Educators must balance experiences in digital and natural worlds to foster children's healthy learning and development. Thus, we next discuss current perspectives on the role of nature and outdoor education in children's development. Essentially, we are returning to views of children's learning and development in the early school years through the lens of the ecological model introduced in Chapter 1; in particular, we strive to bridge informal and formal learning experiences in some of the major microsystems of children's lives (see Figure 5.1).

Figure 5.1   Connecting Learning In and Out of the Classroom

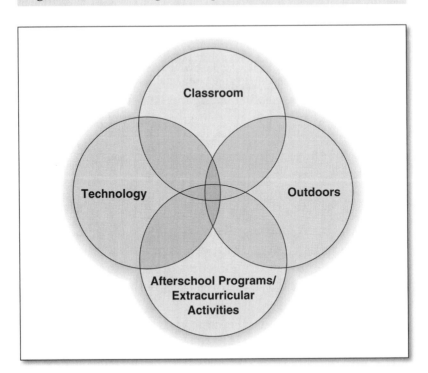

Educational Technology for Children

As we know, children between the ages of 4 and 8 years are developing important cognitive, self-regulation, and social competencies (see Chapter 1). Developmental and educational psychologists emphasize children's need for active interaction with materials and people to support development of these skills. Unfortunately, even today many of the technologies (i.e., television programs, video games) used by children are relatively passive and do not encourage reflection and other kinds of deep intellectual processing (e.g., Greenfield, 2009). Research shows that despite technological developments, children continue to use traditional media for entertainment much more than other technologies that could benefit their learning and development. For example, studies showed that children 2 to 7 years spend an average of 11 minutes using a computer program and more than 3 hours watching television and videos (e.g., Roberts, Foehr, Rideout, & Brodie, 1999); recent reports suggest that the amount of time children spend with media is climbing. The American Academy of Pediatrics suggests that children this age should be limited to 1 to 2 hours maximum of screen time (including television, video games, and computers) per day. Along with concerns about physical health, developmentalists are concerned that extensive time with electronic media discourages children from reading and the cognitive benefits associated with it, such as sustained attention and reflection (e.g., Comstock & Scharrer, 2006), and this might foster impulsivity along with other behavioral and social problems. An examination of the potential negative effects of television and other media is beyond the scope of this book; we probably do not need to remind educators about children's exposure to inappropriate content and extensive use of media. Instead, we concentrate on the constructive uses of interactive media, first by looking at educational television and computer programs and then by considering other technological tools such as those used by the teacher and students in this chapter's *Window Into Practice*. Educators can contribute by revealing, supporting, or creating productive uses of technology for children's learning.

Sandra Calvert (1999), researcher and director of the Children's Digital Media Center, defined an **educational television** or **computer program** as "one designed to teach children academic concepts, such as reading, math, science, history, or geography, that can also be a part of school experiences" (p. 180). These programs are based on curriculum goals which organize and build on age-appropriate concepts. Children under the age of 8 are the age group most likely to use computers for educational programs and games (Becker, 2000). Educational programs are sometimes distinguished from **prosocial programs** which focus on the social and emotional needs of children. Of course, some programs can be both educational and prosocial. For example, educational programs geared for children, such as *Sesame Street*, have been found to have short- and long-term positive influences on children's literacy skills and school adjustment (e.g., Huston & Wright, 1998). These programs were deliberately and carefully planned by child experts and others to foster children's learning and development.

Research on the influences of educational media on children's learning has consistently shown that it is the *quality* of the programs that matter (e.g., Singer & Singer, 2005). In addition, studies show that children's learning with media is enhanced when adults are involved and provide constructive guidance and feedback (e.g., Kirkorian, Wartella, & Anderson, 2008). Features of effective or high quality educational television and computer programs include the following (Calvert, 1999):

> Research on the influences of educational media on children's learning has consistently shown that it is the *quality* of the programs that matter . . . learning with media is enhanced when adults are involved . . .

- *Age-Appropriate Content.* Children understand the information; programs involve concrete lessons (not hidden or abstract) with perceptually salient production techniques (i.e., moderate levels of action, singing, catchy visual and auditory special effects) and comprehensible language.
- *Theme-Based and Repetitive Content.* Each show or program focuses on a particular lesson and repeats important content.
- *Gender and Ethnic-Appropriate Characters.* Children are able to identify with and use characters as models for behavior. Programs present a diverse cast.
- *Familiar Characters and Settings.* Children are more likely to learn from regular watching of programs they like and understand.
- *"Fun" Learning Content.* Programs demonstrate the intrinsic value of learning. Characters are enthusiastic about what they are learning.

- *Interactivity and Multimedia Learning Environments.*
  Children participate in the activity. Even some educational television shows elicit responses from children;
  these can be expanded with accompanying CD-ROM
  games and stories in the home and classroom (e.g., see
  PBS Teachers, Resources).

Teachers can draw upon these features to select appropriate computer programs for classroom learning and for communicating with parents about appropriate educational
programs for their children at home.

Research shows that when used appropriately, computer
programs can help to enhance cognitive, language, and social
skills, as well as learning approaches of children in preschool
and the primary grades. These learning experiences extend
but cannot replace teacher-child and child-child interactions
in the classroom (see Chapter 3). For example, studies show
that when working together on computer programs,
children's attitudes toward learning, spoken communication,
and cooperation levels can increase (see Van Scoter, Ellis, &
Railsback, 2001). Computer play also offers opportunities to
see and explore beyond everyday experiences (e.g., animals in
their habitats, people in different countries), as well as provides unique intellectual experiences, such as representing
actions not possible in the physical world (i.e., manipulating
gravity or speed) and allowing children to discover the result-
ing effects. Importantly, research shows that use of supporting
activities (e.g., manipulatives or real objects) to help children
understand concepts along with computer instruction provides the greatest benefits in problem solving, logical thinking, and concept learning (e.g., Van Scoter et al., 2001). In
addition, learning is best enhanced when technology use is
connected to what children already know and can build upon,
as constructivist educators acknowledge (see Chapter 4).

However, educators need to be cautious about exaggerated
claims about the use of computer programs to promote complex thinking and learning (Greenfield, 2009). Although some
suggest that interactive media (e.g., games, talking books)

have the potential to stimulate more complex learning than other instructional methods because of their interactive nature, research shows mixed findings (Wartella, Caplovitz, & Lee, 2004). Some evidence shows that interactive games can improve children's visual skills (i.e., spatial, iconic, or ability to read images), but little research has revealed their potential for enhancing sophisticated cognitive competencies and learning beyond other teaching methods. Interactive storybooks, for example, do not necessarily evoke better story comprehension than audiovisual presentations. Interactive stories that include elements (clicking on illustrations, icons, etc.) that are integral to the story can aide recall, but incidental elements may interfere with children's understanding of stories. Researchers suggest that interactive technologies may foster children's thinking about strategies to enhance their learning *if* they allow children to structure the activity, adjust the material to their needs and abilities, and receive appropriate feedback (e.g., Calvert, 1999). As we have noted in Chapter 1, children ages 4 to 8 are just beginning to develop abilities to regulate and reflect on their learning experiences and may only benefit from carefully designed programs with adult guidance.

Recent research confirms that executive functioning plays a role in young children's computer use. Recall that **executive functioning** involves abilities to control thinking processes to complete a task, such as holding information in mind (working memory), shifting attention appropriately, and inhibiting irrelevant actions (see Chapter 2). In one study, 4-year-old children with greater executive functioning skills were better able to click the mouse to forward a computer storybook while maintaining comprehension of the story (Lauricella, Barr, & Calvert, 2009). Parents' guidance of these activities provided appropriate scaffolds for their learning. For example, those with children who were apparently able to shift focus from mouse control to the storyline focused on instructions for clicking. If their children had lower executive functioning abilities (difficulty coordinating these activities), parents helped their children attend to the storyline and took control of the mouse themselves. Thus, it is important for educators to be aware of attentional and other skills required for operating computer programs that children are currently developing, so that learning (i.e., story understanding) is possible. Children may not always be able to profit from independent computer use.

Another important question regarding appropriate use of technology by children concerns the use of the Internet as a *tool kit* (Greenfield & Yan, 2006). Most of the research to date focuses on the use of the Internet by adolescents. However, enough research has been done to conclude that age plays a dominant role in children's understanding of the Internet (Yan, 2006). Despite the lack of empirical evidence for the effective use of the Internet by younger children, some preliminary guidelines for use can be offered based on developmental understandings and related research. For example, researchers have repeatedly shown that children under the age of 8 are deceived by advertising, partly because they lack the cognitive skills to understand the motives of the advertiser (Comstock & Scharrer, 2006). Likewise, we would not expect children to be able to question the legitimacy of the sources of information on the Internet; thus, educators must carefully choose appropriate websites tied to the curriculum (Yan, 2006). Similar to criteria for selecting valuable computer programs, developmentally appropriate websites for children include picture menus, meaningful icons, and simple instructions (e.g., auditory for preschoolers), as well as allow some child control and independent exploration. In addition, sites should depict content relevant to children's real-world experiences, as well as various positive social values and models. Of course, educators must pay close attention to Internet safety guidelines (likely included in school policies) and closely monitor children's use in the classroom.

Portable technologies, such as digital cameras, may have the best potential for empowering children to make sense of their classroom experiences. For example, digital photography and journals have been shown to be excellent self-reflection tools in the early grades of school (Wang & Hoot, 2006). Furthermore, as seen in the opening *Window,* these tools provide teachers and

> Portable technologies . . . may have the best potential for empowering children to make sense of their classroom experiences.

parents with opportunities to gain insights into school experiences from children's perspectives and perhaps guidance for extending lessons.

Table 5.1 provides some guidelines based on research for the use of technology with children in preschool through Grade 3 (e.g., Van Scoter et al., 2001). These guidelines are consistent with NAEYC (1996) recommendations for appropriate use of technology with children ages 3 through 8.

Table 5.1 Guidelines for Fostering Learning and Development With Technology

Use of Technology for Fostering Learning and Development	Guidelines for Practice
Provide catalyst for social interaction related to children's work to improve their spoken communication and cooperative skills.	Incorporate computer(s) into typical learning center activities (not in separate computer lab); place in a central location with two chairs at each computer or several computers close together to foster social interaction. Primary Grades: Provide more opportunities for independent use as children develop literacy and computer skills. Teacher becomes more involved as a monitor, guide, and questioner to promote collaborative learning.
Enhance opportunities for developing positive approaches toward learning and views of self competencies.	Provide alternative ways for children to learn and demonstrate learning by choosing programs for individual children that match their interests and attention

	spans (e.g., limiting screens or stimulating noises for those with difficulty concentrating). Use appropriate assistive technologies (e.g., alternate keyboards, Touch Windows) with children with special needs.
Encourage exploration, imagination, and problem solving, and build conceptual learning.	Infuse use of technology into curriculum. Choose software that is open-ended, involves active learning and decision making, and builds on what children already know. Limit use of drill-and-practice software (glorified worksheets). Provide supporting activities (e.g., manipulatives) and experiences (e.g., field trips).
Promote learning for a purpose.	Do things with written language in the real world. For example, children can make labels for dramatic play or write letters with word processing software. Children can also present their work to others using video cameras, PowerPoint, and other technologies.
Promote self-reflection.	Have children take photos of their works in progress and discuss their intentions, strategies, skills developed, plans for improvement, and so forth.
Encourage positive uses of educational programs outside the classroom.	Provide suggestions to parents and children for quality educational television and computer programs and limits for media use.

Many of the suggested uses of technology in Table 5.1 are illustrated in Robert's classroom in the introductory *Window Into Practice*. Gimbert and Cristol (2004) made similar proposals for helping children become technology-literate based on standards developed by the Informational Society for Technology in Education (2007) and guidelines by NAEYC (1996). These authors provided several detailed descriptions of how other early childhood teachers have integrated technology into valuable curriculum units with the assistance of parents and university educators. The following provides snapshots of a few of these units:

- *Preschool.* Curriculum focused on exploring wild animals, initially through a CD-ROM. Supervising adults guided children to select images of animals from a database and create a collage. Children dictated a story about the collage to an adult to type into the computer or narrated their stories into a tape recorder and played it for others. Guided class discussions were incorporated. The teacher videotaped the lessons to share with parents.
- *Kindergarten.* Computers were set up as an activity center for learning about plants. Adults guided small groups of children through steps of a software program that allowed children to create and print drawings of plants. They also recorded a statement about their plant and shared their work with the class.
- *First Grade.* The teacher made use of a WebQuest series of lessons designed to support primary students' technology competency and help them learn about puppetry across cultures. Final tasks included making puppets, writing a play for the puppets using a word processor, and presenting a videotaped puppet show.

—— ✂ ——

...children need a "balanced media diet, one that is not only virtual, but also allows ample time for ... experiences that lead to [other] important qualities of mind."

Gimbert and Cristol (2004) also provided detailed descriptions of first- and second-grade science and math lessons aided by technology. In addition, they emphasized the support needed to assist teachers with infusing technology into developmentally appropriate curriculum.

The Resources section of this book includes specific suggestions, lesson plans, and materials to support these efforts.

In sum, there are a number of constructive uses of interactive media as tools to further young children's learning. However, a number of child experts and researchers warn that children need a balance of other types of learning activities to promote healthy development and well-being (e.g., Crain, 2003; Elkind, 2009; Healy, 1999; Singer & Singer, 2005). For example, Patricia Greenfield (2009), a leading researcher in the field, concluded that children need a "balanced media diet, one that is not only virtual, but also allows ample time for reading and auditory media experiences that lead to [other] important qualities of mind" (p. 71). In particular, she argued that television, video games, and the Internet may help children develop some cognitive skills (i.e., visual intelligence), but the cost might be deep processing: mindful knowledge acquisition, analysis, critical thinking, imagination, and reflection. She pointed to one communication technology that does provide time to reflect and develop critical thinking skills: the written word; indeed, strong research evidence supports the argument that better readers are more reflective and critical thinkers than others. On the other hand, we have seen how electronic media designed for educational purposes can be used as a tool among many others to foster children's learning. Teachers can introduce electronic technologies in connection with real-world, hands-on features of an activity, and allow time for reflection and expressive reporting (Healy, 1999), as Mark in the introductory *Window* demonstrated. Although David Elkind (2009, mentioned at the beginning of this chapter) is a leading advocate for allowing children to develop naturally through play, he also noted the potential value of technology to create a "new educational model"— giving children more of a say and time to engage in valuable learning experiences with teacher guidance and creativity (pp. 202–203). Balance is key; thus, we turn to a brief discussion of the value of another type of learning experience: the outdoors.

OUTDOOR EDUCATION

Few have not heard about "nature-deficit disorder," a term coined by Richard Louv (2008), author of the popular book, *Last Child in the Woods: Saving Our Children From Nature-Deficit Disorder*. Of course, nature-deficit disorder is not an official diagnosis but a way of viewing a problem with what is perceived as our increasing disconnection from nature. Apparently this deficit is a global concern. A recent study showed that most of the mothers from 16 nations reported that their children enjoyed playing outside, but they were concerned that they did not spend enough time doing so (Singer, Singer, D'Agostino, & DeLong, 2009). According to Louv and others, lack of outdoor experiences limits children's development in all domains: physical, cognitive, and social. Although abundant research supports the value of outdoor play for promoting children's physical activity, health, and well-being, less has been devoted to examining influences on other aspects of development in young children. This neglect might be partly due to the belief that it is especially critical for older children to connect to nature (e.g., Montessori, 1966; Sobel, 2008). Nonetheless, we report some of the potential cognitive and social benefits of **outdoor education** for preschoolers and primary-grade children and how early childhood educators can take advantage of these opportunities to promote academic learning. Outdoor education is simply defined as organized learning that takes place outside.

Stephen Kellert (2005) proposed how nature can help foster children's cognitive and emotional development on the basis of the scanty research available. He noted that children's experience with nature may incorporate three types of contact: direct, indirect, and vicarious. *Direct contact* often involves spontaneous interaction with processes of the natural environment that function

...direct experience in the natural world greatly aids young children's emerging capacities to form basic understandings of facts and terms, create simple classifications, and begin to discern causal relationships ...

mostly independent of human control, such as observing, exploring, climbing on, and collecting things in meadows, creeks, forests, or even backyards. *Indirect contact* involves activities in highly managed environments, such as zoos, nature centers, and parks, as well as interactions with pets, house plants, and vegetable gardens. *Vicarious contact* with nature involves experiences with symbolic images, such as representations of animals in media and toys. Psychologists suggest that although vicarious experiences are helpful, they need to be coupled with direct experiences for optimal learning and well-being in childhood and beyond. Kellert asserted that direct experience in the natural world greatly aids young children's emerging capacities to form basic understandings of facts and terms, create simple classifications, and begin to discern causal relationships in the early stages of cognitive development.

He proposed that the natural world affords numerous highly engaging opportunities for children to identify and label objects and discriminate their features and properties, as well as sort and assign them to categories. It also provides multiple opportunities for children to develop abilities to analyze and comprehend facts and ideas as they mature in the next cognitive stage. For example, children may begin to systematically examine empirical evidence encountered in everyday life, such as where plants grow (and not grow), how certain animals behave, when the moon changes, and so on. Kellert (2005) claimed that ". . . no other aspect of a child's life offers this degree of consistent but varied chances for critical thinking and problem solving—a steady diet for the mind as well as the body" (p. 69). Further, he argued that experiences with nature promote children's abilities to receive and respond affectively to information and ideas in their early stages of emotional development; in turn, they are motivated to pursue knowledge. Howard Gardner (1991) also suggested that outdoor education fosters *connected knowing* where education is part of, rather than separate from, life.

Kellert is not alone in his view that nature provides powerful motivational and learning experiences for children. Other psychologists are investigating the notion that exposure to nature in childhood is critical for our learning and

> ... teachers and other adult school personnel also receive many of these benefits from green school environments, making their jobs more pleasurable and productive.

well-being (e.g., Rathunde, 2009; Wells & Lekies, 2006). Although experts may disagree about whether there is a "critical period" for taking advantage of these natural learning opportunities in childhood, many agree about some of the following benefits of direct and indirect experiences with nature (e.g., see Charles, Louv, Bodner, Guns, & Stahl, 2009; Crain, 2003):

- *Stimulates curiosity, powers of observation, and scientific learning.* Children learn the scientific method by patiently observing and pursuing their own questions about wildlife. (See Kellert's explanation, described earlier.)
- *Inspires creativity.* Children are often motivated to draw and write about nature, as well as create opportunities for dramatic play outdoors (e.g., build clubhouses). Research has shown that children are more likely to engage in more creative forms of play in school grounds with natural, green areas (e.g., Bell & Dyment, 2006).
- *Enhances abilities to focus.* Children's attentiveness has been related to greater proximity and daily exposure to natural settings (e.g., Wells, 2000). Children diagnosed with attention deficit/hyperactivity disorder in particular are better able to concentrate and manage their symptoms in and after exposure to greener environments (e.g., Faber Taylor & Kuo, 2008; Kuo & Faber Taylor, 2004).
- *Fosters social skills.* Research documents the social and cognitive benefits of unstructured outdoor play at recess for primary-grade children (see, e.g., Pellegrini & Bohn, 2005). Children tend to play more cooperatively on green than manufactured schoolyards (e.g., Bell & Dyment, 2006).
- *Promotes physical activity.* Several studies indicate that providing outside play at recess for children (at minimum every 60 minutes) encourages physical activity, and it may even have long-term health benefits. For example,

one study showed that children who were more active at age 5 were healthier when they were older, even if their physical activity declined (Janz et al., 2009).

- *Reduces anxiety.* Exposure to green views and access to natural play areas has been linked to reduced stress in children (Wells & Evans, 2003).

It is notable that teachers and other adult school personnel also receive many of these benefits from green school environments, making their jobs more pleasurable and productive.

Recognizing these benefits, there has been a recent and growing movement by educators and others to promote outdoor education, by taking advantage of natural settings near school and recreating natural environments on playgrounds and school grounds (e.g., the *Children and Nature Network,* headed by Richard Louv, and the *Natural Learning Initiative,* headed by Robin Moore). It is important that children have opportunities for unstructured play in these environments, as well as some occasional structured activities tied to the curriculum. Table 5.2 provides some practical ideas for improving playgrounds and utilizing natural outdoor environments for educating young children at school (e.g., Rosenow, 2008; White, 2004).

Of course, teachers cannot transform a dull playground into a more natural, greener, and stimulating setting on their own. But they can encourage community members and school administrators to begin making improvements by discussing the advantages of outdoor education and providing initial referrals to organizations for help. Fortunately, the current movement for outdoor education (i.e., one often hears, "leave no child inside") has inspired a number of dedicated groups to provide resources and support for these efforts. Even without making major renovations, teachers can begin to balance indoor with some outdoor educational activities suggested in Table 5.2. We learned how one teacher in the introductory *Window* incorporated a field trip to an apple farm as part of a curriculum unit that also helped children

Table 5.2 Enhancing Outdoor Educational Environments and Activities

Basic Elements of Natural Play and School Grounds	• Abundant indigenous plant life, including trees, bushes, flowers, and long grasses, with which children can explore and interact • Water • Sand (and water nearby) • Diversity of texture, color, and materials (e.g., rocks) • Animals, bugs, butterflies, creatures in ponds, worm bins • Natural places to sit on or under, climb, provide shelter • Places that offer (limited) privacy, views, and opportunities for socialization • Places to run and play active games • Structures, equipment, and materials that can be changed or adapted for imaginary play • Ways to experience different weather conditions (e.g., cover-ups for rain, warm clothes for snow) • In less ideal concrete areas—wooden planter boxes for growing vegetables and flowers
Developmental Considerations	• It might be most important for children ages 4 to 7 to develop a fondness for the natural world. Model a sense of wonder, curiosity, and sensitivity. • Teach children to love rather than fear nature. Avoid developmentally inappropriate topics such as global warming that are difficult to understand and frightening. • Foster children's curiosity about creatures that they might fear, such as spiders and bees. • Assist children with caring for plants and animals.

Sample Activities	• Allow children to play freely (without adult direction) in natural playground settings for periods of time. • Go on "I spy" walks in natural areas nearby. • Encourage questions, observations, systematic data collection, and other aspects of the scientific method prompted by everyday experiences (e.g., changes in the weather, shade spots, bug activities). • Plant a garden with parent help. • Plan field trips to visit natural environments related to curriculum goals. • Get involved with other educators with interests in nature and outdoor education to gather further ideas, resources, and support (see Resources).

("Basic Elements" section adapted from White, 2004.)

become technologically literate. We return to his class to focus on one child's experience in *The Child's Window*.

The Child's Window

Eva had been a student at Sierra Elementary School since kindergarten. Now she was in the third grade and Mr. Flores was to be her teacher. Eva had known Mr. Flores from the afterschool tutoring program, and she was looking forward to having him as her teacher because his former students talked about how much fun they had in his class. Eva had struggled in school and found it hard to keep up with her work. She didn't have many enriching experiences at home because her mother was working two jobs and her older sister was rarely at home. Eva spent many evenings alone at home trying to make sense of her homework and remembering what the teacher had said that day. Eva had never turned in a book report or any assignment that required going to the library or visiting someplace. The afternoon tutoring hour helped Eva to stay on top of her math and English homework, but Eva didn't understand how to continue the homework once she got home. Eva would often watch the few clear stations on TV, eat a bowl of cereal, and then go to bed with her best friend, Mia, her canine companion since she was 2.

Eva was a little nervous about having a handheld computer assigned to her. She had never been allowed to play with a computer. Some of Eva's classmates had seen this type of technology before, and they worked together to figure it out which made Eva feel a little better. When Mr. Flores assigned Eva to the "interview" team, she was thrilled. Eva had watched the news people on TV and knew she could do a good job coming up with questions for the apple farmer; she remembered picking apples with her grandmother when she was younger. Eva and her classmates talked about the list of questions they would like to ask, and then they consulted with another team to check their understanding of the apple growing process and make sure their questions were fitting. Finally, they discussed who should be the primary interviewer. Eva wanted to do this job more than anything, but she held back from jumping in to volunteer; maybe someone else wanted to be the interviewer. After much discussion, one of Eva's classmates nominated Eva to take the job and all agreed.

As Eva prepared for the interview, she could feel the butterflies in her stomach. She typed her questions into the handheld computer and made sure the recording application was working properly. Her classmate, Ashley, was going to videotape the interview while the others on the team prepared the information for the presentation. Eva was relieved to find the apple farmer to be a calm, tender, old man who loved to talk about his farm. The interview went fairly smooth, with only a small glitch of a few noisy tractors in the background. Eva thanked the farmer for his time and then ran off to join the other students playing in the orchard. They spent the rest of the afternoon enjoying a picnic and exploring the large farm before returning to school.

The next day Eva and her teammates put their interview together using the video camera and the editing software. Eva could not believe her eyes! There she was on the big screen in class, with poise and confidence interviewing the farmer. Could she possibly be a real news reporter when she got older? She wondered. Eva knew that she had a lot to learn about news reporting and that the technology that Mr. Flores had purchased for them could help her research and learn more about the world.

Eva is an example of a child whose experiences are not uncommon today. She spends much of her time after school indoors at home alone, with a television and pet for stimulation. It is fortunate that her teacher has provided enriching experiences in and out of the classroom that connect her to larger natural and social worlds. It is also very fortunate that she has access to an afterschool program to extend her social and academic experiences. Recent research indicates that children in low-income families participate less in afterschool programs and in other important extracurricular activities such as athletics, music lessons, or community clubs (e.g., scouts) than children from more affluent families (e.g., Dearing et al., 2009). This lack of participation is noteworthy because studies have shown clear advantages for children. For example, one longitudinal study showed that children who consistently participated in extracurricular activities during kindergarten and first grade had higher academic achievement scores (i.e., math) at the end of first grade, even after controlling for their prior achievement skills and family backgrounds (NICHD ECCRN, 2004). Notably, these activities were rarely focused on academics. It appears as if extracurricular activities provide enrichment experiences that stimulate intellectual and other developmental processes. Again, diverse learning experiences also appear to be key for optimal learning and development.

Chapter Summary
Balancing Educational Experiences

Today's educators can take advantage of new technologies as well as "old" (natural) settings to expand children's worlds and encourage their love of learning and academic achievement. This chapter focused initially on current concerns with the developmental appropriateness of technology use by young children. Although there is evidence that some children are spending too much time with electronic media at home, currently the potential use of technology in most early childhood classrooms for learning purposes is not realized (e.g., Wang & Hoot, 2006). We offered recommendations for selecting quality educational programs as well as for constructive uses of other technologies in preschool and primary classrooms based on research and case studies. We then turned to another current concern—the lack of contact that many children have with nature. We looked at how psychologists and educators are promoting outdoor education as a way for children to connect to the natural world and stimulate their thinking and well-being. Finally, we repeated the theme that connecting diverse learning experiences in and out of the classroom is optimal for supporting children's development.

Questions to Ponder

1. How do you use technology for educational purposes in your own life? How do these tools promote learning? How might educators help young children reap similar advantages with appropriate modifications for their development?

2. How have your own experiences with nature affected your motivation, learning, and well-being, and your passions as an educator? In what ways can educators share these insights with young children?

Practice Exercises

1. **Infusing Technology in an Early Childhood Classroom.** Create a sample lesson plan with colleagues for a particular grade level that builds children's technological skills and supports their learning (see Table 5.1). For guidance on developmental appropriateness, refer to the *Technology Profile Indicators for Young Children* (PreK–2; International Society for Technology in Education, 2007) and to the NAEYC (1996) position statement on *Technology and Young Children—Ages 3 through 8*. (Also, see Resources, NETC: Early Connections).

2. **Connecting to Learning Outside the Classroom.** Ask children about their learning experiences outside the classroom, and think of ways to foster this learning.

a. What opportunities do children have for learning from educational media, nature, extracurricular activities? How can teachers build on these experiences in the classroom?

b. Do some children have limited out-of-school learning experiences? If so, how can valuable experiences be integrated into classrooms, field trips, or after-school programs? How can parents be supported to provide these experiences for their children? One way might be to gather information about free or low-cost opportunities in the community (consider transportation) to share with parents through newsletters, conferences, or open houses.

Key Words

Digital divide

Educational television or computer programs

Prosocial programs

Executive functions (see Chapter 2)

Outdoor education

Conclusion

Our goal in *A Developmental Approach to Educating Young Children* is to provide prospective and practicing preschool and primary teachers with a brief introduction to current thinking about the development and education of children based on research and theory. Children from 4 to 8 years are developing important skills, behaviors, and attitudes toward learning during the early years of school that nudge them toward more or less optimal pathways. This is a time when children are moving from early to middle childhood ways of thinking, feeling, and behaving, not necessarily in a straightforward fashion. They are not always easy to understand and predict; careful observation and patience is essential for getting to know children. As in any important developmental transition, this is a time when strengths and vulnerabilities acquired from earlier life play a powerful role in children's adjustment to new experiences and demands—in this case, different school settings. Thus, educators' sensitivity and attunement to children's needs, interests, and development are especially critical as well as fruitful during these years. This is a time when children's most important relationships continue to be with adults. Thus, the adults closest to children—teachers, parents, other caregivers—need to work together to facilitate their adjustment and take advantage of their emerging capacities and enthusiasm for learning. This is a time when children are also developing more sophisticated social awareness and skills that allow them to enhance friendships as well as expand relationships with peers in general. Thus, they need opportunities and support for relating to peers to ensure that they will care about and participate effectively in the learning community at school; otherwise, they probably will not. This is a time when children are still developing abilities to regulate their behavior and are beginning to consciously regulate their thoughts and strategies. Thus, teachers need to provide well-managed classroom routines and activities that allow children to feel comfortable and plan ways to approach learning tasks on their own, as well as with others. This is a time when children are developing important concepts about their world and begin formal learning in subjects that adults deem essential for their adaptation and eventual abilities to contribute to it. Thus, it is important for teachers to utilize instructional strategies that are effective in promoting skills (i.e., math, literacy) as well as thinking processes (i.e., scientific, creative) that will lead children to develop meaningful understandings and incite them to learn more. Taking advantage of opportunities available through technology as well as through direct contact with the natural world is important. Implementing contemporary educational approaches espoused here is difficult. Teachers cannot do it alone; they need assistance, resources, and continuous support. They also need affirmation and signs that they are helping their students learn and develop in positive ways.

In this little book, we have provided some general recommendations for improving practice from contemporary developmental perspectives to aid in this endeavor. Other books in the *Classroom Insights* series will provide more specific recommendations for supporting children's learning of subject matter and skills, as well as attend to individual and cultural differences. In Resources, we have provided a list of resources and professional organizations to support teachers in their everyday lives in school. In addition, we have provided a list of inspiring stories written by or about teachers who are attuned to children and courageous enough to share their struggles and achievements vividly and honestly. We hope that these resources for and affirmations of developmentally appropriate practices help, but we know that they are not enough.

From our experiences working with teachers, we have noted three major obstacles to implementing developmentally appropriate practices in preschools and primary grades today. We have also seen teachers successfully circumvent these obstacles and hopeful signs that some obstacles might dissipate with continued advocacy. The first is the obvious tension teachers feel between implementing practices that they believe are appropriate for children and what they are urged to do to promote academic achievement in the name of the No Child Left Behind act (NCLB) or by parents; these tensions in the United States are real and must be acknowledged. Fortunately, these concerns have been recognized by child experts, professional organizations, policymakers, and others. For example, a number of books have been published and public statements made recently about the increased focus on academics and reduction of playtime in schools, such as Elkind's (2009) *The Power of Play* and the Alliance for Childhood report titled, "Crisis in Kindergarten: Why Children Need to Play in School" (Miller & Almon, 2009). And tireless advocacy efforts by organizations, such as the National Educational Organization, to modify NCLB appear to be gaining support.

The second obstacle, related to the first, is that many people in the United States simply do not know much about child development and the implications of this knowledge for education. Misunderstandings are still prevalent, such as "early learning is better" because young children easily "absorb" information, and "sitting still" and following directions promote good behavior and learning. These misunderstandings lead to inappropriate expectations for classroom practices. Therefore, teachers may feel like they have to battle others to implement developmentally appropriate practices. It is interesting that standard early educational practices in other countries that are often revered for excellent academic achievement, such as Japan, appear to be fairly in line with what American developmental and educational psychologists advocate. For example, Japanese educators pay much more attention to helping children develop socioemotional skills and relationships through play than to academic instruction in the early school years (e.g., Lewis, 1995; Tobin et al., 2009). Perhaps current concerns with catching up with student achievements in other countries, especially in science and math, will point us to examine beliefs about children's development and early educational practices in other countries as well as in our own. Such reexamination might help others to realize the benefits of approaches that patiently nurture children's development across domains to enhance academic learning and life skills.

The third obstacle is that implementing the kinds of practices advocated here is challenging and time-consuming, especially for inexperienced teachers. It requires support from administrators, resources, and time to discuss and reflect on practices with colleagues and mentors (e.g., Ritchie & Crawford, 2009). In addition, it requires understanding of child development (Chapters 1 & 2), and how to balance child- and teacher-directed practices (Chapter 4), establish positive relationships (Chapter 3), and deal with a host of other responsibilities along with helping children move toward established learning standards. Some of these standards need reexamination. We do not have to compromise high quality practices for high standards (*if* they are appropriate), but we might have to educate others about what quality practices look like for young children. Fortunately, we have professional organizations like NAEYC and others to turn to for clear explanations and examples that can be shared with others.

Although implementing developmentally appropriate practices is challenging, it is highly rewarding. Educators are more likely to elicit children's cooperation, enthusiasm, engagement, and "wonderful intellectual ideas" with contemporary, constructivist approaches than with more traditional approaches (e.g., Duckworth, 1996). They will spend less time correcting misbehavior and having to coerce children to do schoolwork, tasks that drain energy and passions for teaching. We believe that greater implementation of and support for the practices advocated here will help to entice and retain the enthusiastic, intelligent educators needed for guiding children toward positive pathways through school and life.

Resource A

Tools for Reflection and Improvement

A.1 CONTEMPORARY AND TRADITIONAL TEACHER BELIEFS ABOUT CHILDREN AND APPROPRIATE PRACTICES

(From Table 1.2)

Use the table to reflect on your beliefs about children and appropriate practices in the early school years. Put a + to note the items you strongly support and a − to note those you do not support.

Do you endorse more practices in the Contemporary or Traditional section? Or do you endorse a mix of practices? What factors do you think have contributed to your beliefs?

+/−	Contemporary Beliefs	+/−	Traditional Beliefs
	• Addressing children's social, emotional, and physical needs is just as important to learning as meeting their intellectual needs.		• The most important job as a teacher is to help students meet well-established standards; basic academic skills should be the teacher's top priority. Children should be retained if they have not mastered basic skills at grade level.
	• One of the best ways children learn is through active exploration in an environment prepared by teachers.		• Children learn best through repetition and practice.
	• Children's enthusiasm for a task is more important than how well they do.		• Teachers should emphasize quality in final products.
	• Seeing things from children's perspectives is key to their learning and good performance in school.		• Giving rewards and extra privileges for good performance is one of the best ways to motivate children to learn.
	• Creating caring relationships with children is critical for their learning.		
	• To maximize learning, teachers need to help children reflect on and discuss their thoughts and feelings.		• During a lesson, children should not be able to interrupt a teacher to relate personal experiences.

	• Subject areas should be related to each other and children's real experiences and participation in concrete activities.		• Instruction should be clearly divided into separate subject areas.
	• Children are able to participate in setting classroom rules.		• One of the most important things to teach children is how to follow rules and to do what is expected of them in the classroom.
	• Children should be able to choose alternative ways of approaching planned activities.		
	• Curriculum should respond primarily to individual differences in ability and interest.		• Curriculum should respond primarily to grade-level expectations.
	• Opportunities for interacting with peers and teachers in small groups should predominate over whole group and individual experience.		• For most of the time, children should be expected to work quietly on their own and in teacher-led small reading groups.
	• Teacher observation and informal assessments are the most valid way to gauge children's learning and performance.		• Tests are the most valid way to assess children's performance.
	• Teachers should deal with parents mainly informally, encouraging them to participate in the classroom and at home.		• Teachers should deal with parents mainly through formally scheduled meetings and conferences.

A.2 Children's Approaches
to Learning in the Classroom

(From Table 2.1)

Think of a child in a classroom, and check each of the behaviors that describe this child. Next add descriptors of your own.

To what extent does this child reflect positive or negative approaches toward learning? What might enhance the child's positive approaches?

Orientation/Attitudes Toward School

- Laughs or smiles easily
- Approaches the teacher comfortably
- Approaches new activities with enthusiasm
- Is curious and eager to learn
- Is optimistic and recovers from setbacks quickly (sees the glass "half full")

_____

_____

On-Task Involvement/Engagement in Class Activities

- Listens carefully to teacher's instructions
- Responds promptly to teacher's requests
- Uses classroom materials responsibly
- Shows interest in activities
- Returns to selected activities after interruptions
- Sticks to task at hand, even during longer or unpleasant tasks
- Participates in group activities

_____

_____

Other Work Habits

- Seeks challenges
- Persists in the face of difficulties
- Asks for help when needed
- Follows classroom procedures
- Works well independently
- Makes plans to reach goals
- Anticipates consequences of behaviors
- Works toward goals
- Uses time wisely

_____

_____

Social Behavior (Regulation)

- Waits turn to talk in class when appropriate
- Does not disrupt others
- Does not get into fights

_____

_____

A.3 Promoting Self-Regulation in Preschool and Primary-Grade Classrooms

(From Table 2.2)

Check each of the practices observed in a classroom.
  How many "promoting" activities were observed? How might more be incorporated? Which practices would you choose to focus on first? Why?

Emotional Regulation (ER)

- Be a role model for how to express and regulate emotions, such as calming down before reacting or seeking help when frustrated.
- Encourage children to label emotions and identify causes and consequences of emotions in everyday activities.
- Discuss emotions with children. Label and identify causes and consequences of emotions during class meetings (circle times) and story discussions. (Many lessons, books, and props are available.)
- Intentionally instruct children in how to handle emotions. These strategies might include using self-talk to calm down, reframing the problem, identifying alternative actions, seeking help from others, and avoiding problem situations.
- Use validated methods designed to help children control negative emotions. Encourage children to relax, reflect on feelings, and then decide how to react to the cause of their feelings.
- Get involved in dramatic and role-playing activities with children.

Cognitive and Behavioral Regulation (Executive Function [EF] and Effortful Control [EC])

- Provide a variety of learning activities that are challenging, meaningful, and require active participation.
- Involve children in establishing clear guidelines for classroom behavior and consistently apply these guidelines.
- Encourage children's self-talk to guide behavior (i.e., compliment themselves) and solve academic problems.
- Implement discovery-based learning.
- Allow children to derive and share multiple ways of solving academic problems (e.g., addition, manipulating objects, and estimating).

Self-Directed Learning (Planning, Goal Setting, Strategy Use)

- Give children increasing responsibility for conducting challenging work on their own or with classmates.
- Let children design or choose how to complete some learning tasks.
- Ask children to talk about their plans in advance, using prompts like "what else . . ." and "remember when . . ." to connect to previous scripts for completing tasks.
- Support children's independent learning efforts.
- Help children set realistic, short-term goals and provide feedback about their progress.
- Provide specific information about strategies to remember, plan, and improve their work.
- Encourage autonomous help-seeking behavior. Provide hints, cues, or questions to assist after children have tried on their own (expert scaffolding).
- Help children figure out when they do and do not have the skills and resources to accomplish tasks.
- Create opportunities for children to engage in "reciprocal teaching," taking turns with the teacher and classmates to model the task process.

Responsible Decision Making (Social Behavior)

- Help children solve problems and make decisions by identifying issues (e.g., fair play on the playground), generating goals to guide decisions, thinking of alternative solutions and consequences, selecting the best solution, and making final plans (Kress & Elias, 2006).
- Refer to validated methods for social problem solving; check the Collaborative for Academic, Social, and Emotional Learning (CASEL) organization.

A.4 Helping Children Become Less Inhibited in the Early Grades of School

(See Chapter 2, Children at Risk for Adjustment Difficulties)

Incorporate one or more of these practices in a classroom. Keep a reflective journal noting growth or changes in children. Share your experience with a colleague.

- **Encourage children to speak more often** through subtle and less controlling conversational forms.
- **Play games** in which children are required to take speaking turns, and subtly praise (e.g., by smiling) shy children for speaking.
- **Encourage gradual participation in class discussions** by asking shy children questions they can respond to (even if it is just their names).
- **Establish personal relationships with shy children** by having private conversations with them about their families or out-of-school experiences.
- **Gently encourage shy children to interact with other children** in the classroom; start by pairing them with more sociable classmates.
- **Prepare shy children** for changes in the routine or special events.
- **Allow shy children to participate** in cross-age tutoring and play groups.
- **Encourage interactions** in thoughtfully designed cooperative learning groups in the classroom.

(Adapted from Coplan & Arbeau, 2008.)

A.5 Preoverschool to Kindergarten Transition

(See Chapter 2, Readiness of the School)

Which of the following transition practices have you seen incorporated at a school? How have children and their families benefited? What other transitional practices might be added to facilitate adjustment?

- Prekindergarten children visit a kindergarten class.
- The prekindergarten teacher visits a kindergarten class.
- The kindergarten teacher visits a preschool class.
- The school holds a spring kindergarten orientation for prekindergarten children.
- The school holds a spring kindergarten orientation for prekindergarten children's parents.
- There is a schoolwide activity for prekindergarten children.
- Teachers hold individual meetings with parents about kindergarten.
- Teachers share written records about children's prekindergarten experience with elementary school teachers.
- Teachers contact the kindergarten teacher about curriculum and/or specific children.

A.6 TEACHER-CHILD RELATIONSHIP INTERVIEW QUESTIONS

(From Table 3.1)

Answer the following questions regarding your relationship with a specific child.

Then reflect on the following:

- o *How would you describe the quality of this relationship?*
- o *How might this relationship be improved?*

Question	Responses
Choose three words that describe your relationship with _____ *child's name.* For each word, tell me a specific experience or time that describes that word.	1. 2. 3.
Tell me about a specific time you can think of when you and ___ "clicked." How did you feel? How do you think _____ felt?	
Tell me about a specific time you can think of when you and _____ really weren't "clicking."	
What gives you the most satisfaction being _____'s teacher? Why?	
Every teacher has at least occasional doubts about whether s/he is meeting a child's needs. What brings this up for you and ____? How do you handle these doubts?	
What is your relationship like with _____'s family? (Sample questions from the Teacher Relationship Interview, Pianta, 1999.)	

A.7 PROMOTING POSITIVE TEACHER-CHILD RELATIONSHIPS

(See Chapter 3)

▌ *Reflect on the recommendations, and choose one you would like to accomplish. How would you follow through with this recommendation?*

- Reflect on individual relationships with children. Attend to those that may not yet be close or positive.
- Help children develop emotional regulation skills so that they are better able to form positive interpersonal relations with others, including teachers.
- Create frequent opportunities in classroom routines for positive teacher-child interactions that children can anticipate.
- Ensure that individual children have regular "unconditional" opportunities to develop positive relationships with a stable teacher (employ "Banking Time").

"Banking Time" principles (adapted from Pianta, 1999):

  (a) Children are told that the time is theirs to do what they wish; teachers follow and participate as children direct.
  (b) The sessions occur on a predictable basis, and participation is *not* contingent on children's behavior.
  (c) The teacher is neutral and objective and does not focus on children's performance or skills.
  (d) The teacher draws attention to a few relationship messages (e.g., "I accept you," "You are important," "I am available," "I am consistent," "I am helpful when asked").

- Consider how previous relationships or stressors affect relationships with children. Obtain support from mentors or other school professionals when needed.
- Respect and value children as human beings; take their ideas seriously and show interest in their personal lives outside school.
- Expect positive behavior and work from children; hold them to developmentally appropriate standards.
- Ensure that children are not humiliated; avoid embarrassing or making sarcastic remarks about them (young children are likely to take remarks literally).
- Let children know that there is no risk of disapproval or rejection when they do poorly on their work; praise them when attempting challenging work even when they fail.

A.8 Children's Peer Relations in Preschool and the Primary Grades

(See Chapter 3, Child-Child Relationships in School)

Select three different children. Check the behaviors that indicate they are developing positive peer relationships at school.

Which children appear to be developing positive peer relationships? Why?

Which children appear to need some support? Why?

What can you do to help children build social skills and support their relationships with peers?

Child #1:	• Being a member of a group (e.g., sharing, listening, taking turns, cooperating, being considerate, being helpful, handling disputes) • Initiating interactions • Resolving conflicts without fighting (e.g., learning to compromise) • Understanding justifiable self-defense • Demonstrating empathy toward peers (e.g., showing emotional distress when others suffer, becoming aware of others' experiences or perspective-taking, helping rather than hurting or neglecting, supporting rather than dominating, respecting rather than belittling others)
Child #2	• Being a member of a group (e.g., sharing, listening, taking turns, cooperating, being considerate, being helpful, handling disputes) • Initiating interactions • Resolving conflicts without fighting (e.g., learning to compromise) • Understanding justifiable self-defense • Demonstrating empathy toward peers (e.g., showing emotional distress when others suffer, becoming aware of others' experiences or perspective-taking, helping rather than hurting or neglecting, supporting rather than dominating, respecting rather than belittling others)

| *Child #3:* | • Being a member of a group (e.g., sharing, listening, taking turns, cooperating, being considerate, being helpful, handling disputes)
• Initiating interactions
• Resolving conflicts without fighting (e.g., learning to compromise)
• Understanding justifiable self-defense
• Demonstrating empathy toward peers (e.g., showing emotional distress when others suffer, becoming aware of others' experiences or perspective-taking, helping rather than hurting or neglecting, supporting rather than dominating, respecting rather than belittling others)

(Elias et al., 1997) |

A.9 Promoting Healthy Peer Relations

(See Chapter 3, Child-Child Relationships in School)

Observe the following teacher behaviors associated with promotion of healthy peer relationships in a classroom. Provide an example of each of the practices.

Rate the extent to which these practices are demonstrated from a teacher's view, using a 1 to 5 scale (1 = not at all, 5 = frequently). (Practicing teachers can rate their own practices.)

Which behavior or practice could be improved? How?

	I attend to my own interactions with children as a model for my students.
	I ensure that all children are included in small group activities and prompt children when needed.
	I take advantage of everyday social conflicts to discuss and resolve together in class meetings.
	I strive to implement child-centered, developmentally appropriate practices in my classroom.
	I allow some free time in class and at recess for children to interact with minimal adult control (adults observe and monitor from a distance).

	I encourage friendships in the classroom and allow friends to work together on academic tasks at times.
	I initiate structured games on the playground (provide materials and guidance, then let children go).
	I watch out for bullying behavior.
	I implement a social skills curriculum shown to be effective.

A.10 Promoting Family Involvement

(See Chapter 3, Teacher-Parent Relationships and Family Involvement in School)

Which practice do you feel confident implementing? How have you implemented it or would you do so?

Which area do you feel least confident implementing? How might you gather support or resources to help build these practices?

Parenting	• Help families establish home environments to support children as students. (Expected outcomes include strengthening children's attachment to school and their parents' confidence in parenting. Teachers also gain understanding and respect for families' strengths.)
Communicating	• Design effective forms of school-to-home and home-to-school communications about school activities and children's experiences. (Expected outcomes include increasing children's understanding of their roles as students and their parents' monitoring of their progress. Teachers also gain access to parent networks for communications.)
Volunteering	• Recruit and organize parent help and support. (Expected outcomes include enhancing children's skill in communicating with adults and parents' understanding of the teacher's job. Teachers also gain time to provide individual attention to children, with volunteers assisting in the classroom.)
Learning at home	• Provide ideas about how families can help children with homework and other school-related activities. (Expected outcomes include enhancing children's attitudes toward schoolwork and parents' awareness of their children as learners. Teachers also gain respect for family time.)
Decision making	• Include parents in school decisions. (Expected outcomes include increasing children's positive experiences as a result of improved policies, and parents' feelings of ownership of school. Teachers become better aware of parent perspectives.)

Collaborating with the community	• Identify and integrate community resources and services to strengthen school programs, family practices, and children's learning and development. (Expected outcomes include enhancing children's skills and talents through enriched experiences, and parents' use of needed services. Teachers become better aware of resources to enrich curriculum and services to refer families when needed.)
(Sample activities adapted from Epstein et al., 2002.)	

A.11 Creating Partnerships With Parents and Families

(From Table 3.4)

Consider each of the following values in creating partnerships with parents.

Choose one value, and briefly outline how you might incorporate supportive practices.

If possible, implement your plan and record observations of family responses in a reflective journal.

Partnership Values	Practical Suggestions
Create a warm, welcoming school and classroom atmosphere for parents to visit and participate.	• Welcome and communicate with parents using positive and relaxed body language, facial expressions, and tone of voice. • Provide a choice of activities for parents (e.g., a parent may feel more comfortable decorating bulletin boards than reading to students). • Create a parent resource room or space for parents to connect. • Address parents by name and find out some details about their lives and interests. • Spend time outside class getting to know parents (e.g., invite them to stay for lunch, come early for coffee, etc.).
Model positive communication behavior such as active listening and conflict resolution skills.	• Keep eye contact and maintain an open posture (e.g., don't cross your arms, sit behind your desk, etc.) when talking. • Listen with the intention of "checking in" to make sure parents' concerns are heard (e.g., "I can see that you are worried about your child's progress and stress level. Can you tell me more about why you are concerned?"). • Use language translators whenever there is a language barrier or when parents feel more comfortable communicating in their native language.

Partnership Values	Practical Suggestions
Commit to ongoing two-way communication channels that become part of the school and classroom culture.	• Distribute routine notes, memos, or photos about classroom news. • Provide a central place in the classroom where parents can go for more information. • Use the Internet, e-mail, and homework webpage to communicate ideas, events, quotes for the week, and so forth. • Incorporate home visits, especially for transitions to elementary school. • Use parent surveys to solicit input on various classroom practices, and identify their talents, skills, and availability.
Provide avenues of respect and sensitivity for parents to express their goals, choices, and concerns about their children. (Values adapted from Copple & Bredekamp, 2009.)	• Value and model these beliefs. • Reflect (write about) your feelings about parents and potential conflicts. • Seek out a trusted mentor educator to discuss feelings and ideas.

A.12 POSITIVE CLASSROOM CLIMATES

(From Table 4.1)

Observe a classroom, and check each of the qualities demonstrated. What recommendations would you make for improving the climate of this classroom?

Teacher Qualities	Examples
Enthusiasm	Uses facial expressions to show happiness and tone of voice to communicate excitement about classroom activities.
Enjoyment	Smiles often and regards challenges as opportunities to grow.
Connection	Makes eye contact with children and responds to comments and questions in a pleasant tone.
Responsiveness	Invites children to ask questions and validates opinions with a response (verbally and nonverbally).
Security	Demonstrates fairness and respect for each individual child (consistency). Does not show favoritism. Keeps in confidence the feelings and personal comments made by children.
Classroom Qualities	Examples
Variety and Choice	• Many "interest" centers organized around recent learning themes • Soft, cozy places for reading or quiet activities • Spaces for group work and collaboration (i.e., desks arranged in groups) • Manipulatives accessible and labeled for use • Child-directed, "hands-on" (sensory) learning materials available • Photographs and recent work from the children displayed around the classroom

Classroom Qualities	Examples
Movement	• Ample space for movement and accessible to disabled children • Furnishings in good repair and free from causing injury or inhibiting movement • Room to walk between learning areas
Physical Space	• Child-sized furnishings and décor • Lots of natural light in the classroom • Good ventilation • Clean and organized spaces • Well-maintained equipment and furnishings

A.13 Constructivist Classroom Organization

(From Table 4.2)

Add examples of constructivist management practices to the table below. Then observe practices in a classroom. Does this classroom appear to incorporate constructivist practices? or a mix of practices? How do these practices appear to influence children's approaches to learning?

	Examples	Add Examples
Productivity	• Children work in small groups with specific tasks to accomplish. • The teacher moves around the classroom providing feedback and attention to keep children engaged. • The teacher encourages peer conversations about the stories at the reading center. • Children have a sense of ownership of the classroom rules and feel a sense of responsibility to uphold those rules. • Children are engaged in "jobs" which support classroom routines.	
Behavior Management	• Children participate in creating classroom rules (i.e., "no talking bad about your classmate"). • The teacher uses role-playing to foster interpersonal skills and manage conflict. • The teacher uses both positive and negative consequences depending on the behavior. The tone is calm and nonthreatening. • The teacher models expected behavior such as "inside tone" of voice, manners, and listening to students. • Children work individually or in small groups with plenty of follow-up activities to choose from when they are finished.	

	Examples	Add Examples
Instructional Format	• The teacher provides challenging and meaningful assignments and lessons. • The teacher responds to children's interest in a particular topic and expands the activity to include time to explore their interests. • Children are able to choose materials they prefer to complete a project. • The teacher provides a variety of reading levels while encouraging students to choose books just beyond their current skill level. • The teacher provides time to engage in meaningful play opportunities.	

A.14 Quality Instructional Practices

(See Chapter 4, Classroom Instruction)

Observe a classroom teacher and provide examples of how that teacher demonstrates the following practices.

Attending to individual skill levels and making adjustments as needed.
Examples:
Providing an extension of lessons for children who are ready to move ahead.
Examples:
Basing lessons on children's prior knowledge.
Examples:
Rotating learning centers and books to keep children interested and curious.
Examples:
Keeping lessons and activities relevant to a child's world.
Examples:

A.15 Thinking About the "Learners" in a Classroom

(From Table 4.3)

Plan a learning activity/lesson for preschoolers or primary-grade children, and address the following questions in your plans.

Would you consider yourself a "learner-centered" teacher? Why or why not?

Questions	Responses
How many children would be interested in this current activity?	
Which children need another avenue for learning this activity? How will I choose an alternative activity for these children?	
Is there a new skill that the children are learning in this activity?	

(Continued)

Questions	Responses
What other impacts on learning might this activity have?	
How can I relate this activity to the children's lives and make it relevant?	
Is there a change in our classroom schedule that needs adjustment to accommodate this learning? If so, how might this change in schedule impact the rest of the school day?	
How might I engage those children that seem to have difficulty with this activity? (Adapted from Rogoff, Turkanis, & Bartlett, 2001.)	

A.16 GUIDELINES FOR FOSTERING LEARNING AND DEVELOPMENT WITH TECHNOLOGY

(From Table 5.1)

Plan a curriculum unit for a particular grade level (or combination) using the following guidelines for practice. Look to the sample lessons/units briefly described in Chapter 5.

Use of Technology for Fostering Learning and Development	Guidelines for Practice
Provide catalyst for social interaction related to children's work to improve their spoken communication and cooperative skills.	Incorporate computer(s) into typical learning center activities (not in separate computer lab); place in a central location with two chairs at each computer or several computers close together to foster social interaction. Primary Grades: Provide more opportunities for independent use as children develop literacy and computer skills. Teacher becomes more involved as a monitor, guide, and questioner to promote collaborative learning.
Enhance opportunities for developing positive approaches toward learning and views of self-competencies.	Provide alternative ways for children to learn and demonstrate learning by choosing programs for individual children that match their interests and attention spans (e.g., limiting screens or stimulating noises for those with difficulty concentrating). Use appropriate assistive technologies (e.g., alternate keyboards, Touch Windows) with children with special needs.
Encourage exploration, imagination, and problem solving, and build conceptual learning.	Infuse use of technology into curriculum. Choose software that is open-ended, involves active learning and decision making, and builds on what children already know. Limit use of drill-and-practice software (glorified worksheets). Provide supporting activities (e.g., manipulatives) and experiences (e.g., field trips).

(Continued)

(Continued)

Use of Technology for Fostering Learning and Development	Guidelines for Practice
Promote learning for a purpose.	Do things with written language in the real world. For example, children can make labels for dramatic play or write letters with word processing software. Children can also present their work to others using video cameras, PowerPoint, and other technologies.
Promote self-reflection.	Have children take photos of their works in progress and discuss their intentions, strategies, skills developed, plans for improvement, etc.
Encourage positive uses of educational programs outside the classroom.	Provide suggestions to parents and children for quality educational television and computer programs and limits for media use.

A.17 ENHANCING OUTDOOR EDUCATIONAL ENVIRONMENTS AND ACTIVITIES

(From Table 5.2)

Option 1: Evaluate the grounds of a school and surrounding areas for inclusion of basic natural elements, and make a list of elements that might be easy and difficult to add. Begin with the "easy" list and consider how to use existing resources to begin making improvements.

Option 2: Plan a developmentally sensitive outdoor learning activity.

Basic Elements of Natural Play and School Grounds ("Basic Elements" section adapted from White, 2004.)	• Abundant indigenous plant life, including trees, bushes, flowers, and long grasses, with which children can explore and interact • Water • Sand (and water nearby) • Diversity of texture, color, and materials (e.g., rocks) • Animals, bugs, butterflies, creatures in ponds, worm bins • Natural places to sit on or under, climb, provide shelter • Places that offer (limited) privacy, views, and opportunities for socialization • Places to run and play active games • Structures, equipment, and materials that can be changed or adapted for imaginary play • Ways to experience different weather conditions (e.g., cover-ups for rain, warm clothes for snow) • In less ideal concrete areas—wooden planter boxes for growing vegetables and flowers
Developmental Considerations	• It might be most important for children ages 4 to 7 to develop a fondness for the natural world. Model a sense of wonder, curiosity, and sensitivity. • Teach children to love rather than fear nature. Avoid developmentally inappropriate topics such as global warming that are difficult to understand and frightening. • Foster children's curiosity about creatures that they might fear, such as spiders and bees. • Assist children with caring for plants and animals.

(Continued)

(Continued)

Sample Activities	• Allow children to play freely (without adult direction) in natural playground settings for periods of time. • Go on "I spy" walks in natural areas nearby. • Encourage questions, observations, systematic data collection, and other aspects of the scientific method prompted by everyday experiences (e.g., changes in the weather, shade spots, bug activities). • Plant a garden with parent help. • Plan field trips to visit natural environments related to curriculum goals. • Get involved with other educators with interests in nature/outdoor education to gather further ideas, resources, and support (e.g., *Children & Nature Network*).

Resource B

Professional Organizations and Model Programs

This section introduces educators and other child professionals to exemplary organizations and programs that are based on contemporary perspectives of child development and current research and provides specific recommendations for effective practices in preschool and the primary grades. Note that the website addresses given here are current as of April 2010.

Organizations and Centers

National Association for the Education of Young Children (NAEYC)

http://www.naeyc.org/

NAEYC provides a framework for best practice, taking into account recent research and leading early childhood professionals' core understanding of how children develop and learn best. This organization is the leading voice for excellence and equity in educating young children. The practical guidelines outlined in each developmental stage provide the early childhood educator with the tools necessary to meet children's needs. NAEYC also provides a standard of excellence in qualifying what makes a teacher successful in early childhood education.

American Psychological Association Center for
Psychology in Schools and Education (APA CPSE)

http://www.apa.org/ed/schools/cpse/index.aspx

The American Psychological Association is a professional scientific organization representing over 150,000 psychologists from around the world. The APA CPSE provides research in a variety of areas including teacher needs, classroom management, evidence-based practice, diversity issues, school processes, and support for children and families through the school process.

Collaborative for Academic, Social,
and Emotional Learning (CASEL)

http://www.casel.org/home.php

The CASEL provides summaries of scientific and evidence-based understandings of social and emotional learning. The CASEL views social and emotional learning as a vital part of educational practice and provides information on teacher training, relevant research, assessment, leadership development, policy, and communication through an educational lens.

UCLA Center for Mental Health in Schools

http://smhp.psych.ucla.edu/

This organization assists in supporting school and community links to provide social service programs to children in school. The center is primarily interested in social-emotional learning and advocates for the protective factors that support student resiliency and reduce risk. The center addresses problems that interfere with school success, such as physical and mental health, poor school adjustment, low attendance, substance abuse, emotional upset, and violence.

Family Involvement Network of Educators (FINE)

http://www.hfrp.org/family-involvement

The Family Involvement Network of Educators is part of the Harvard Family Research Network, which provides information, research, and involvement projects to facilitate support for families to be actively involved in children's learning. Available resources include teaching tools, training methods, research reports, and many family involvement projects available for participation.

Center on the Social and Emotional Foundations
for Early Learning (CSEFEL)

http://www.vanderbilt.edu/csefel/

This organization provides resources and evidence-based practices for early care educators, programs, and health providers. The center is funded by the Office of Head Start and Child Care Bureau.

Center for Research on Education,
Diversity & Excellence (CREDE)

http://crede.berkeley.edu/research/crede/index.html

The Center for Research on Education, Diversity & Excellence is connected to the Graduate School of Education at the University of California, Berkeley, and it is focused on improving educational practices for students with challenges created by language or cultural barriers or poverty. The CREDE Five Standards for Effective Pedagogy are described in detail, and research and resources to support the standards are provided.

Children's Digital Media Center,
Georgetown University

http://cdmc.georgetown.edu/

Children's Digital Media Center consists of a five-university consortium of scholars, researchers, educators, policymakers, and industry professionals. The goal of the center is to improve children's digital media and how this media affects children's social adjustment, academic achievement, and personal identity.

PBS Teachers

http://www.pbs.org/teachers/

The Public Broadcast System for Teachers provides practical, multimedia resources for P–12 educators. The website features lessons plans and activities on a wide range of topics and issues and online activities. Teachers will find areas of colleague discussions, collaboration of resources, and professional development opportunities.

Early Connections: Technology in Early Childhood Education, Northwest Educational Technology Consortium (NETC)

http://www.netc.org/earlyconnections/

This website provides information and resources pertaining to the appropriate and effective use of technology for young children. The content sponsors of the website discontinued funding as of 2005; however, valuable publications and information are still available.

Children & Nature Network (C&NN)

http://www.childrenandnature.org/

The Children and Nature Network supports children's connections to nature by providing a worldwide network of organizations and individuals dedicated to the health and well-being benefits of children experiencing the natural environment. The website provides updated news briefs, publications, and research and resources in the form of books and videos. There are opportunities to become involved in the peer-to-peer collaboration between researchers, educators, individuals, and organizations.

Model Programs/Curriculum

Comer School Development Program (SDP)

http://info.med.yale.edu/comer/

The Comer Process is a comprehensive K–12, research-based educational reform program. The program is described as an "operating system" in which three school teams create, assess, and modify a comprehensive school plan with a common goal to maximize positive classroom climate and provide an optimal learning environment for students and teachers.

Providing Alternative Thinking Strategies (PATHS)

http://www.prevention.psu.edu/projects/PATHS.html

This curriculum is designed for counselors and educators for developing self-control, emotional awareness, and relational problem-solving skills in children. The systematic developmental procedure supports social competence and understanding in children while facilitating the educational process in the classroom.

Responsive Classroom

http://www.responsiveclassroom.org/prodevelop/schoolwideimple.html

Responsive Classroom is a schoolwide and classroom practice (approach) which enhances the social, emotional, and academic growth in elementary children. Through the fundamental belief that children need both academic and social-emotional skills, the Responsive Classroom approach has been shown to increase student learning, motivation, and responsibility and decrease negative behaviors.

Second Step

http://www.cfchildren.org/programs/ssp/overview/

Second Step is a program for preschool through eighth grade, which focuses on the social-emotional development of children. Developed by the Committee for Children, Second Step advocates research-based instruction intended to cover social-emotional issues such as empathy, impulse, personal safety, problem-solving skills, and anger management skills for children.

The Incredible Years

http://www.incredibleyears.com/program/teacher.asp

The Incredible Years provides parent and teacher training programs to address social competence and reduce aggression in children. This school and community-based program supports intervention tools based on the theory that children have multiple interacting factors (individual, family, community) which contribute to potential risk and/or protective measures that influence social competence.

Olweus Bullying Prevention Program

http://www.olweus.org/public/index.page

The Olweus Bullying Prevention Program offers several specific components for long-term prevention and reduction of bullying in schools. Through this research-based, school-wide approach, the program seeks to improve peer relations by implementing systematic activities and information throughout schools, classrooms, and communities wherever children are present.

Bridging Cultures Project

http://www.wested.org/cs/we/view/pj/26

This project provides an information framework for understanding and preventing cultural conflicts between students at school. The available publications are designed to stimulate questions and support ethnographic research and are not designed as a "how to" curriculum. The project has stimulated international workshops, supported research, and provided information for preservice teachers as well as veteran educators, school administrators, and community politicians.

Big Math for Little Kids

http://www.njn.net/education/teachers/bigmathforlittlekids/

Big Math for Little Kids is an online teacher training program for early education teachers, designed to enhance math content and knowledge through teaching strategies, which will provide a foundation for success in later, more rigorous mathematics in elementary and high school years.

Resource C

Recommended Reading

Stories From the Classroom

Duckworth, E. (1996). *"The having of wonderful ideas" and other essays on teaching and learning*. New York: Teachers College Press.

Duckworth, E. (2001). *"Tell me more": Listening to learners explain*. New York: Teachers College Press.

Lewis, C. (1995). *Educating hearts and minds: Reflections on Japanese preschool and elementary education*. Cambridge, MA: Harvard University Press.

Nicholls, J., & Hazzard, S. (1992). *Education as adventure: Lessons from second grade*. New York: Teachers College Press.

Paley, V. (1992). *You can't say you can't play*. Cambridge, MA: Harvard University Press.

Paley, V. (2000). *White teacher*. Cambridge, MA: Harvard University Press.

Paley, V. (2005). *A child's work: The importance of fantasy play*. Cambridge, MA: Harvard University Press.

Rogoff, B., Turkanis, C., & Bartlett, L. (2001). *Learning together: Children and adults in a school community*. New York: Oxford University Press.

Teaching Tolerance Project. (1997). *Starting small: Teaching tolerance in preschool and the early grades*. Retrieved from http://www.tolerance.org/

Tobin, J., Ysueb, Y., & Karasawa, M. (2009). *Preschool in three cultures revisited*. Chicago: University of Chicago Press.

Guides for Practice

Bodrova, E., & Leong, D. (2007). *Tools of the mind: The Vygotskian approach to early childhood education* (2nd ed.). Upper Saddle River, NJ: Pearson Education.

Copple, C., & Bredekamp, S. (2009). *Developmentally appropriate practice in early childhood programs: Serving children from birth through age 8*. Washington, DC: National Association for the Education of Young Children.

Elias, M., & Butler, L. (2006). *Social decision making/social problem solving: A curriculum for academic, social, and emotional learning.* Champaign, IL: Research Press.

Elias, M., Zins, J., Weissberg, R., Frey, K., Greenberg, M., Haynes, N., et al. (1997). *Promoting social and emotional learning: Guidelines for educators.* Alexandria, VA: Association for Supervision & Curriculum Development.

Epstein, J., Sanders, J., Simon, B., Salina, K., Jansorn, N., & Van Voorhis, F. (2002). *School, family, and community partnerships* (2nd ed.). Thousand Oaks, CA: Corwin.

Good, T., & Brophy, J. (2008). *Looking in classrooms* (10th ed.). Boston: Allyn & Bacon.

McCombs, B., & Whisler, J. (1997). *The learner-centered classroom and school: Strategies for increasing student motivation and achievement.* San Francisco: Jossey-Bass.

Pianta, R. (1999). *Enhancing relationships between children and teachers.* Washington, DC: American Psychological Association.

Stipek, D. (2002). *Motivation to learn: Integrating theory and practice* (4th ed.). Boston: Allyn & Bacon.

Glossary

5 to 7 Developmental Shift. The change in children's thinking, behavior, and relationships as a result of the dynamic interplay between their developing abilities to make sense of their thoughts, feelings, and changing worlds, and the ways in which these worlds stimulate and respond to them.

Approaches to Learning. A broad range of skills or dispositions that influences children's learning and adjustment; includes school-related attitudes, engagement in activities, persistence, and work habits.

Attachment Theory. A developmental theory stipulating that the quality of attachment a child has to one or more caregivers (affective relationship) influences feelings of security and trust and subsequent relationships; Bowlby's theory.

Classroom Climate. The social and emotional atmosphere of the classroom.

Classroom Instructional Support. Classroom practices which support learning processes and curriculum goals.

Classroom Organization. Management of classroom activities, including routines, behaviors, and instructional formats that influence student engagement.

Close Relationship. A relationship characterized by warmth, open communication, and appropriate dependency.

Conflicted Relationship. A relationship between individuals who are often at odds and show little affection for each other.

Constructivist. An educational approach based on ideas that children must "construct" their own knowledge and understanding of the world. Teachers guide the process of learning through creating learning activities and focusing attention, posing questions, and stretching children's thinking.

Dependent Relationship. A relationship in which one individual (e.g., child) is overly reliant on the other (e.g., teacher), and interactions are often emotionally negative.

Developmentally Appropriate Practices (DAP). A phrase used to describe teaching strategies, curriculum, discipline practices, learning approaches, classroom environments, and interpersonal relationships that promote children's development at all ages.

Digital Divide. The unequal access to computer technologies among children from different income groups.

Domains of Readiness. Related to self-regulation, domains of readiness include executive functioning, emotional regulation, and approaches to learning. Skills in these domains affect many aspects of children's learning and development in school.

Ecological Perspective. View of development attending to children's interactions and relationships with others in multiple environmental contexts, based on Bronfenbrenner's ecological model.

Educational Television or Computer Programs. Programs intentionally designed to teach children academic concepts.

Effortful Control (EC). Efficient management of one's thought processes.

Emotional Regulation (ER). Management of the intensity of emotional responses such as anger, fear, pleasure, or sadness appropriate for the situation.

Executive Function (EF). The ability to control thinking processes to complete a task, such as holding information in mind (working memory), shifting attention appropriately, and inhibiting irrelevant actions.

Learner (Child)-Centered Practices. Educational practices based on understandings of developmental and psychological processes. Involves the teacher assuming a "facilitator" or "partner" role and encouraging children to take responsibility for their learning.

Memory Strategies. A conscious effort (plan of action) to encode or recall information from memory to achieve a goal, for example, plans to remember where a favorite toy is located.

Outdoor Education. Organized learning that takes place outside.

Playful Learning. Enjoyable guided play that appears spontaneous and encourages academic exploration and learning.

Profiles of School Readiness. Subgroups of children displaying similar patterns of strengths and weaknesses across domains of competence (i.e., cognitive, social, behavioral).

Prosocial Programs. Programs that focus on the social and emotional needs and skills of children and encourage positive behavior.

Reactive Aggression. An aggressive response that is easily provoked by irritation or perceived or actual threats.

Reciprocal Teaching. A group discussion between students and the teacher (or adult) designed to strengthen comprehension skills. Teachers and students take turns being the discussion leader, and students learn how to monitor their understanding of what they are reading through dialogue.

Reticent Behavior. Approach-avoidant behavior often manifested in prolonged onlooker behavior.

Scaffolding. The process by which adults provide support to a child who is learning to master a task or problem by performing or directing those elements of the task that are beyond the child's ability.

School Adjustment. Indicators of children's adjustment to school are attitudes and emotional experiences, involvement and engagement with activities, and performance.

School Readiness. Often refers to the skills and knowledge that children bring to school that are associated with later adjustment and achievement. Current focus is on the provision of supports within schools for fostering children's adjustment and learning.

Self-Reflection. The ability to reflect upon one's own thoughts, emotions, and attributes, such as asking, "Am I doing this right?"

Self-Regulation Skills. Children's ability to manage their emotions, focus their attention, and inhibit some behaviors while engaging in goal-directed behavior.

Social Competence. Socially adaptive behavior, especially with peers.

Social-Constructivist. An approach to learning and teaching based on Vygotsky's theory of development. Children participate in a wide range of activities with teachers and peers as they jointly construct understandings.

Teacher-Directed Practices. Activities, instructional practices, and classroom accommodations planned and implemented by the teacher.

Theories of Mind. Children's intuitive or developing psychological theories about mental states, such as beliefs, intention, desires, and emotions. Children develop abilities to compare their own unobservable thoughts, desires, and beliefs with others.

Working Models. The child's expectation of a relationship based on previous experiences.

Zone of Proximal Development. The gap between what children can do on their own and what they can do with assistance from others, based on Vygotsky's notion.

References

Becker, J. (2000). Who's wired and who's not: Children's access to and use of computer technology. *The Future of Children: Children and Computer Technology, 10,* 44–75.

Bell, A., & Dyment, J. (2006). *Grounds for action: Promoting physical activity through school ground greening in Canada.* Retrieved from http://www.childrenandnature.org/downloads/PHACreport.pdf

Betts, L., & Rotenberg, K. (2007). The development of a short-form of the Teacher Rating Scale of School Adjustment. *Journal of Psychoeducational Assessment, 25,* 150–164.

Birch, S., & Ladd, G. (1997). The teacher-child relationships and children's early school adjustment. *Journal of School Psychology, 35,* 61–79.

Blair, C. (2002). School readiness: Integrating cognition and emotion in a neurobiological conceptualization of children's functioning at school entry. *American Psychologist, 57,* 111–127.

Blair, C., Knipe, H., Cummings, E., Baker, D., Gamson, D., Eslinger, P., et al. (2007). Developmental neuroscience approach to the study of school readiness. In R. Pianta, M. Cox, & K. Snow (Eds.), *School readiness & the transition to kindergarten in the era of accountability* (pp. 149–174). Baltimore: Paul H. Brookes.

Bodrova, E., & Leong, D. J. (2007). *Tools of the mind. The Vygotskian approach to early childhood education.* Upper Saddle River, NJ: Pearson Merrill Prentice Hall.

Boekaerts, M. (2006). Self-regulation and effort investment. In K. A. Renninger & I. Sigel (Vol. Eds.) and W. Damon & R. Lerner (Eds.), *Handbook of child psychology volume 4: Child psychology in practice* (6th ed., pp. 345–373). Hoboken, NJ: Wiley.

Bogard, K., & Takanishi, R. (2005). PK–3: An aligned and coordinated approach to education for children 3 to 8 years old. *SRCD Social Policy Report, 19*(3), 3–21.

Bowlby, J. (1969). *Attachment and loss: Vol. 1. Attachment.* New York: Basic Books.

Bronfenbrenner, U. (1979). *The ecology of human development: Experiments by nature and design.* Cambridge, MA: Harvard University Press.

Bronfenbrenner, U., & Morris, P. (1998). The ecology of developmental processes. In W. Damon (Gen. Ed.) & R. Lerner (Vol. Ed.), *Handbook of child psychology: Vol. 1. Theoretical models of human development* (pp. 993–1028). Hoboken, NJ: Wiley.

Brophy, J. E., & Good, T. L. (1986). Teacher behavior and student achievement. In M. C. Wittrock (Ed.), *Handbook of research on teaching* (3rd ed., pp. 328–375). New York: Macmillan.

Brown, A. (1997). Transforming schools into communities of thinking and learning about serious matters. *American Psychologist, 52,* 399–413.

Brown, A., & Campione, J. (1990). Communities of learning and thinking, or a context by any other name. In D. Kuhn (Ed.), *Developmental perspectives on teaching and learning thinking skills* (pp. 108–126). Basel, Switzerland: Karger.

Calvert, S. (1999). *Children's journeys through the information age.* Boston: McGraw-Hill.

Center for Research on Education, Diversity & Excellence. (CREDE, 2010). *The CREDE five standards for effective pedagogy and learning.* Retrieved from http://crede.berkeley.edu/research/crede/standards

Chandler, M., & Lalonde, C., (1996). Shifting to an interpretive theory of mind: 5- to 7-year olds' changing conceptions of mental life. In A. Sameroff & M. Haith (Eds.), *The five to seven shift: The age of reason and responsibility* (pp. 111–140). Chicago: University of Chicago Press.

Charles, C., Louv, R., Bodner, L., Guns, B., & Stahl, D. (2009). *Children and nature 2009: A report on the movement to reconnect children to the natural world.* Retrieved from http://www.childrenandnature.org/downloads/CNNMovement2009.pdf

Cole, M., Cole, S., & Lightfoot, C. (2005). *The development of children* (5th ed.). New York: Worth.

Comer, J. (2004). *Leave no child behind: Preparing today's youth for tomorrow's world.* New Haven, CT: Yale University Press.

Comstock, G., & Scharrer, E. (2006). Media and popular culture. In K. A. Renninger & I. Sigel (Vol. Eds.) and W. Damon & R. Lerner (Eds.), *Handbook of child psychology, volume 4: Child psychology in practice* (6th ed., pp. 817–858). Hoboken, NJ: Wiley.

Coplan, R., & Arbeau, K. (2008). The stresses of a "brave new world": Shyness and school adjustment in kindergarten. *Journal of Research in Childhood Education, 22*, 377–389.

Copple, C., & Bredekamp, S., (2009). *Developmentally appropriate practice in early childhood programs. Serving children from birth through age 8.* Washington, DC: National Association for the Education of Young Children.

Crain, W. (2003). *Reclaiming childhood: Letting children be children in our achievement-oriented society.* New York: Times Books.

Daniels, D. (2009, April). *The role of motivational characteristics and preschool experiences in children's adjustment to kindergarten.* Paper presented at the biennial meeting of the Society for Research in Child Development, Denver, CO.

Daniels, D., & Perry, K. (2003). "Learner-centered" according to children. *Theory into Practice, 42,* 102–108.

Daniels, D., & Shumow, L. (2003). Child development and classroom teaching: A review of the literature and implications for educating teachers. *Applied Developmental Psychology, 23,* 495–526.

Dearing, E., Wimer, C., Simpkins, S., Lund, T., Bouffard, S., Caronongan, P., et al. (2009). Do neighborhood and home contexts help explain why low-income children miss opportunities to participate in activities outside of school? *Developmental Psychology, 45,* 1545–1562.

Dockett, S., & Perry, B. (2004). What makes a successful transition to school? Views of Australian parents and teachers. *International Journal of Early Years Education, 12,* 217–230.

Dodge, K., Laird, R., Lochman, J., Zelli, A., & Conduct Problems Prevention Research Group. (2002). Multidimensional latent-construct analysis of children's social information processing patterns: Correlations with aggressive behavior problems. *Psychological Assessment, 14,* 60–73.

Dodge, K., Lochman, J., Harnish, J., Bates, J., & Pettit, G. (1997). Reactive and proactive aggression in school children and psychiatrically impaired chronically assaultive youth. *Journal of Abnormal Psychology, 106,* 37–51.

Doherty, R. W., & Hilberg, R. S. (2007). Standards for effective pedagogy, classroom organization, English proficiency, and student achievement. *The Journal of Educational Research, 101*(1), 24–34.

Duckworth, E. (1996). *"The having of wonderful ideas" and other essays on teaching and learning.* New York: Teachers College Press.

Duncan, G., Dowsett, C., Claessens, A., Magnuson, K., Huston, A., Klebanov, P., et al. (2007). School readiness and later achievement. *Developmental Psychology, 43,* 1428–1446.

Dweck, C. (2002). The development of ability conceptions. In A. Wigfield & J. Eccles (Eds.), *The development of achievement motivation* (pp. 57–88). San Diego, CA: Academic Press.

Elias, M., & Butler, L. (2006). *Social decision making/social problem solving: A curriculum for academic, social, and emotional learning.* Champaign, IL: Research Press.

Elias, M., Zins, J., Weissberg, R., Frey, K., Greenberg, M., Haynes, N., et al. (1997). *Promoting social and emotional learning: Guidelines for educators.* Alexandria, VA: Association for Supervision & Curriculum Development.

Elkind, D. (1976). *Child development and education: A Piagetian perspective.* New York: Oxford University Press.

Elkind, D. (2009). *The power of play: Learning what comes naturally.* Cambridge, MA: De Capo Press.

Epstein, J., Sanders, M., Simon, B., Salinas, K., Jansorn, N., & Van Voorhis, F. (2002). *School, family, and community partnerships: Your handbook for action.* Thousand Oaks, CA: Corwin.

Erdley, C., & Asher, S. (1996). Children's social goals and self-efficacy perceptions as influences on their responses to ambiguous provocation. *Child Development, 67,* 1329–1344.

Erikson, M., & Pianta, R. (1989). New lunchbox, old feelings: What kids bring to school. *Early Education and Development, 1,* 35–49.

Faber Taylor, A., & Kuo, F. (2008). Children with attention deficits concentrate better after a walk in the park. *Journal of Attention Disorders, 12,* 402–409.

Gardner, H. (1991). *The unschooled mind: How children think and how schools should teach.* New York: Basic Books.

Gazelle, H., & Ladd, G. (2003). Anxious solitude and peer exclusion: A diathesis-stress model of internalizing trajectories in childhood. *Child Development, 74,* 257–278.

Gimbert, B., & Cristol, D. (2004). Teaching curriculum with technology: Enhancing children's technological competence during early childhood. *Early Childhood Education Journal, 31,* 207–216.

Good, T. L., & Brophy, J. E. (2007). *Looking into classrooms* (10th ed.). Boston: Allyn & Bacon, Pearson Education, Inc.

Greenes, C., Ginsburgh, H., & Balfanz, R. (2004). Big math for little kids. *Early Childhood Research Quarterly, 19,* 159–166.

Greenfield, P. (2009). Technology and informal education: What is taught, what is learned. *Science, 323,* 69–71.

Greenfield, P., & Yan, Z. (2006). Children, adolescents, and the Internet: A new field of inquiry in developmental psychology. *Developmental Psychology, 42,* 391–394.

Haith, M., & Sameroff, A. (1996). The 5 to 7 year shift: Retrospect and prospect. In A. Sameroff & M. Haith (Eds.), *The five to seven shift: The age of reason and responsibility* (pp. 435–449). Chicago: University of Chicago Press.

Halgunseth, L. (2009). Family engagement, diverse families, and early childhood education: An integrated review of the literature. *Young Children, 64,* 56–60.

Hamre, B., & Pianta, R. (2001). Early teacher-child relationships and the trajectory of children's school outcomes through eighth grade. *Child Development, 72,* 625–638.

Hamre, B., & Pianta, R. (2004). Self-reported depression in nonfamilial caregivers: Prevalence and associations with caregiver behavior in child care settings. *Early Childhood Research Quarterly, 19,* 297–318.

Hamre, B. K., & Pianta, R. C. (2007). Learning opportunities in preschool and early elementary classrooms. In R. C. Pianta, M. J. Cox, & K. Snow (Eds.), *School readiness, early learning and the transition to kindergarten* (pp. 49–83). Baltimore: Paul H. Brookes.

Harms, T., Clifford, R. M., & Cryer, D. (1998). *The early childhood environment rating scale: Revised edition.* New York: Teachers College Press.

Harter, S. (1996). Developmental changes in self-understanding across the 5 to 7 shift. In A. Sameroff & M. Haith (Eds.), *The five to seven shift: The age of reason and responsibility* (pp. 207–236). Chicago: University of Chicago Press.

Harter, S. (2006). The self. In K. A. Renninger & I. Sigel (Vol. Eds.) and W. Damon (Eds.), *Handbook of child psychology, volume 4: Child psychology in practice* (6th ed., pp. 505–526). Hoboken, NJ: Wiley.

Healy, J. (1999). *Endangered minds: Why children don't think and what we can do about it.* New York: Simon & Schuster.

Hirsch-Pasek, K., Golinkoff, R., Berk, L., & Singer, D. (2009). *A mandate for playful learning in preschool: Presenting the evidence.* New York: Oxford University Press.

Howes, C., Hamilton, C., & Phillipsen, L. (1998). Stability and continuity of child-caregiver and child-peer relationships. *Child Development, 69,* 418–426.

Howes, C., Matheson, C., & Hamilton, C. (1994). Maternal, teacher, and child care history correlates of children's relationships with peers. *Child Development, 63,* 879–892.

Howes, C., Phillipsen, L., & Peisner-Feinberg, C. (2000). The consistency and predictability of teacher-child relationships during the transition to kindergarten. *Journal of School Psychology, 38,* 113–132.

Howes, C., & Ritchie, S. (2002). *A matter of trust: Connecting teachers and learners in early childhood classrooms.* New York: Teachers College Press.

Hughes, J., Cavell, T., & Wilson, V. (2001). Further support for the developmental significance of the quality of the teacher-student relationship. *Journal of School Psychology, 39,* 289–302.

Huston, A., & Wright, J. (1998). Mass media and children's development. In K. A. Renninger & I. Sigel (Vol. Eds.) and W. Damon (Ed.), *Handbook of child psychology, volume 4: Child psychology in practice* (5th ed., pp. 999–1058). Hoboken, NJ: Wiley.

Hyson, M., Copple, C., & Jones, J. (2006). Early childhood development and education. In K. A. Renninger & I. Sigel (Vol. Eds.) and W. Damon & R. Lerner (Eds.), *Handbook of child psychology, volume 4: Child psychology in practice* (6th ed., pp. 3–47). Hoboken, NJ: Wiley.

International Society for Technology in Education. (ISTE, 2007). *National Educational Technology Standards (NETS) for Students 2007 Profiles Grades PK–2.* Retrieved from http://www.iste.org/Content/NavigationMenu/NETS/ForStudents/2007Standards/Profiles/NETS_for_Students_2007_Profiles.htm

Izard, C. (2002). Translating emotional theory and research into preventive interventions. *Psychological Bulletin, 128,* 796–824.

Janowsky, J., & Carper, R. (1996). Is there a neural basis for cognitive transitions in school-age children? In A. Sameroff & M. Haith (Eds.), *The five to seven shift: The age of reason and responsibility* (pp. 33–63). Chicago: University of Chicago Press.

Janz, K., Kwon, S., Letuchy, E., Gilmore, J., Burns, T., Torner, J., et al. (2009). Sustained effect of early physical activity on body fat mass in older children. *American Journal of Preventive Medicine, 37,* 35–40.

Kagan, S., & Neville, P. (1996). Combining endogenous and exogenous factors in the shift years: The transition to school. In A. Sameroff & M. Haith (Eds.), *The five to seven shift: The age of reason and responsibility* (pp. 387–406). Chicago: University of Chicago Press.

Kail, R. (2000). Speed of information processing: Developmental changes and links to intelligence. *Journal of School Psychology, 38,* 51–61.

Kellert, S. (2005). *Building for life: Designing and understanding the human-nature connection.* Washington, DC: Island Press.

Kellert, S. (2009). Guest introduction: Children and nature. *The Journal of Developmental Processes, 4,* 3–5.

Kirkorian, H., Wartella, E., & Anderson, D. (2008). Media and young children's learning. *The Future of Children, 18,* 39–61.

Konold, T., & Pianta, R. (2005). Empirically-derived, person-oriented patterns of school readiness in typically-developing children: Description and prediction to first-grade achievement. *Applied Developmental Science, 9,* 174–187.

Kress, J., & Elias, M. (2006). School-based social and emotional learning programs. In K. A. Renninger & I. Sigel (Vol. Eds.) and W. Damon & R. Lerner (Eds.), *Handbook of child psychology, volume 4: Child psychology in practice* (6th ed., pp. 592–620). Hoboken, NJ: Wiley.

Kuo, F., & Faber Taylor, A. (2004). A potential natural treatment for attention-deficit/hyperactivity disorder: Evidence from a national study. *American Journal of Public Health, 94*(9), 1580–1586.

Ladd, G. (1996). Shifting ecologies during the 5 to 7 period: Predicting children's adjustment during the transition to grade school. In A. Sameroff & M. Haith (Eds.), *The five to seven shift: The age of reason and responsibility* (pp. 363–387). Chicago: University of Chicago Press.

Ladd, G., Buhs, E., & Seid, M. (2000). Children's initial sentiments about kindergarten: Is school liking an antecedent of early childhood participation and achievement? *Merrill-Palmer Quarterly, 46,* 255–279.

Ladd, G., Herald-Brown, S., & Reiser, M. (2008). Does chronic classroom peer rejection predict the development of children's classroom participation during the grade school years? *Child Development, 79,* 1001–1015.

Lambert, N., & McCombs, B. (1998). *How students learn: Reforming schools through learner-centered education.* Washington, DC: American Psychological Association.

Lauricella, A., Barr, R., & Calvert, S. (2009). Emerging computer skills: Influences of young children's executive functioning abilities and parental scaffolding techniques in the US. *Journal of Children and Media, 3,* 217–233.

Lengua, L., Honorado, E., & Bush, N. (2006). Contextual risk and parenting as predictors of effortful control and social competence in preschool children. *Journal of Applied Developmental Psychology, 28,* 40–55.

Lewis, C. (1995). *Educating hearts and minds: Reflections on Japanese preschool and elementary education.* Cambridge, MA: Harvard University Press.

LoCasale-Crouch, J., Mashburn, A., Downer, J., & Pianta, R. (2008). Pre-kindergarten teachers' use of transition practices and children's adjustment to kindergarten. *Early Childhood Research Quarterly, 23,* 124–139.

Louv, R. (2008). *Last child in the woods: Saving our children from nature-deficit disorder.* Chapel Hill, NC: Algonquin Press.

McClelland, M., Cameron, C., Connor, D., Farris, C., Jewkes, A., & Morrison, F. (2007). Links between behavioral regulation and preschoolers' literacy, vocabulary, and math skills. *Developmental Psychology, 43,* 947–959.

McCombs, B., Daniels, D., & Perry, K. (2008). Children's and teachers' perceptions of learner-centered practices and motivation: Implications for early schooling. *The Elementary School Journal, 109,* 16–35.

McCombs, B., & Whisler, J. (1997). *The learner-centered classroom and school: Strategies for increasing student motivation and achievement.* San Francisco: Jossey-Bass.

McCombs, B. L., & Miller, L., (2007). *Learner-centered classroom practices and assessments.* Thousand Oaks, CA: Corwin.

Miller, E., & Almon, M. (2009). *Crisis in kindergarten: Why children need to play in school.* Retrieved from http://www.allianceforchildhood.org/sites/allianceforchildhood.org/files/file/kindergarten_report.pdf

Montessori, M. (1966). *The secret of childhood.* New York: Ballantine.

National Association for the Education of Young Children. (NAEYC, 1996). *Technology and young children—Ages 3 through 8: A position statement of the NAEYC.* Retrieved from http://www.naeyc.org/files/naeyc/file/positions/PSTECH98.PDF

National Institute of Child Health and Human Development Early Child Care Research Network. (NICHD ECCRN, 2002). Early child care and children's development prior to school entry. *American Educational Research Journal, 39,* 581–593.

National Institute of Child Health and Human Development Early Child Care Research Network. (NICHD ECCRN, 2003). Social functioning in first grade: Associations with earlier home and child care predictors and with current classroom experiences. *Child Development, 74*(6), 1639–1662.

National Institute of Child Health and Human Development Early Child Care Research Network. (NICHD ECCRN, 2004). Are children's developmental outcomes related to before- and after-school arrangement? Results from the NICHD study of early child care. *Child Development, 75,* 280–295.

National Institute of Child Health and Human Development Early Child Care Research Network. (NICHD ECCRN, 2005). A day in third grade: A large-scale study of classroom quality and teacher and student behavior. *The Elementary School Journal, 105,* 305–323.

Nelson, K. (1996). Memory development from 4 to 7 years. In A. Sameroff & M. Haith (Eds.), *The five to seven shift: The age of reason and responsibility* (pp. 141–160). Chicago: University of Chicago Press.

Paley, V. (1992). *You can't say you can't play.* Cambridge, MA: Harvard University Press.

Paley, V. (2000). *White teacher.* Cambridge, MA: Harvard University Press.

Pellegrini, A. (1988). Elementary-school children's rough-and-tumble play and social competence. *Developmental Psychology, 24,* 802–806.

Pellegrini, A., & Blatchford, P. (2000). *The child at school: Interactions with peers and teachers.* London: Arnold Publishers.

Pellegrini, A., & Bohn, C. (2005). The role of recess in children's cognitive performance and school adjustment. *Educational Researcher, 34,* 13–19.

Piaget, J. (1926). *The language and thought of the child.* New York: Harcourt, Brace, & Company.

Piaget, J. (1960). *The psychology of intelligence.* Paterson, NJ: Littlefield, Adams, & Company.

Pianta, R. (1999). *Enhancing relationships between children and teachers.* Washington, DC: American Psychological Association.

Pianta, R. (2004). Schools, schooling, and developmental psychopathology. In D. Cicchetti & D. Cohen (Eds.), *Developmental psychopathology. Vol. 1: Theory and methods* (2nd ed., pp. 494–529). Hoboken, NJ: Wiley.

Pianta, R., & Cox, M. (2002). *Transition to kindergarten*. Early Childhood Research and Policy Briefs. Retrieved from http://www.fpg.unc.edu/ ncedl/PDFs/TranBrief.pdf

Pianta, R., Cox, M., & Snow, K. (2007). *School readiness & the transition to kindergarten in the era of accountability*. Baltimore: Paul H. Brookes.

Pianta, R., La Paro, K., & Hamre, B. (2008). *Classroom assessment scoring system (CLASS)*. Baltimore: Paul H. Brookes.

Ponitz, C., McClelland, M., Jewkes, A., Connor, C., Farris, C., & Morrison, F. (2008). Touch your toes! Developing a direct measure of behavioral regulation in early childhood. *Early Childhood Research Quarterly, 23*, 141–158.

Pressley, M., & McCormick, C. (2007). *Child and adolescent development for educators*. New York: Guilford Press.

Ramey, S., & Ramey, C. (1994). The transition to school: Why the first few years matter for a lifetime. *Phi Delta Kappan, 76*, 194–198.

Rathunde, K. (2009). Nature and embodied education. *The Journal of Developmental Processes, 4*, 70–80.

Raver, C., Garner, P., & Smith-Donald, R. (2007). The roles of emotional regulation and emotion knowledge for children's academic readiness: Are the links causal? In R. Pianta, M. Cox, & K. Snow (Eds.), *School readiness & the transition to kindergarten in the era of accountability* (pp. 121–148). Baltimore: Paul H. Brookes.

Reid, R., Trout, A., & Schartz, M. (2005). Self-regulation interventions for children with attention deficit/hyperactivity disorder. *Council for Exceptional Children, 71*, 361–377.

Rimm-Kaufman, S., Curby, T., Grimm, K., Nathanson, L., & Brock, L. (2009). The contribution of children's self-regulation and classroom quality to children's adaptive behaviors in the kindergarten classroom. *Developmental Psychology, 45*, 958–972.

Rimm-Kaufman, S., & Pianta, R. (2000). An ecological perspective on the transition to kindergarten: A theoretical framework to guide empirical research. *Journal of Applied Developmental Psychology, 21*, 491–511.

Rimm-Kaufman, S., & Pianta, R. (2005). Family-school communication in preschool and kindergarten in the context of a relationship-enhancing intervention. *Early Education and Development, 16*, 287–307.

Ritchie, S., & Crawford, G. (2009). *Issues in preK–3rd education: Time is of the essence (#5)*. Chapel Hill: The University of North Carolina at Chapel Hill, FPG Child Development Institute, First School.

Roberts, D., Foehr, U., Rideout, V., & Brodie, M. (1999). *Kids and media and the new millennium*. Menlo Park, CA: Kaiser Family Foundation.

Rogoff, B., Turkanis, C., & Bartlett, L. (2001). *Learning together: Children and adults in a school community*. New York: Oxford.

Rosenow, N. (2008, January). *Teaching and learning about the natural world: Learning to love the earth and each other*. Retrieved from http://www.naeyc.org/files/yc/file/200801/BTJNature Rosenow.pdf

Rubin, K., Bukowski, W., & Parker, J. (2006). Peer interactions, relationships, and groups. In N. Eisenberg (Ed.), *Handbook of child psychology: Social, emotional, and personality development* (6th ed., pp. 571–645). Hoboken, NJ: Wiley.

Rudasill, K., Rimm-Kaufman, S., Justice, L., & Pence, K. (2006). Temperament and language skills as predictors of teacher-child relationship quality in preschool. *Early Education and Development, 17*, 271–291.

Ryan, R., & Deci, E. (2000). Self-determination theory and the facilitation of intrinsic motivation, social development, and well-being. *American Psychologist, 55*, 68–78.

Sameroff, A., & Haith, M. (1996). Interpreting developmental transitions. In A. Sameroff & M. Haith (Eds.), *The five to seven shift: The age of reason and responsibility* (pp. 3–17). Chicago: University of Chicago Press.

Schneider, S., & Pressley, M. (1997). *Memory development between two and twenty* (2nd ed.). Mahwah, NJ: Erlbaum.

Schneider, W., & Bjorklund, D. (1998). In W. Damon (Editor-in-Chief) & D. Kuhn & R. Sigler (Vol. Eds.), *Handbook of child psychology: Vol. 2* (5th ed., pp. 467–522). Hoboken, NJ: Wiley.

Schulting, A., Malone, P., & Dodge, K. (2005). The effect of school-based kindergarten transition policies and practices on child academic outcomes. *Developmental Psychology, 41*, 860–871.

Siegler, R. (1998). *Children's thinking* (3rd ed.). Upper Saddle River, NJ: Prentice Hall.

Siegler, R., & Alibali, M. (2005). *Children's thinking* (4th ed.). Upper Saddle River, NJ: Prentice Hall.

Sigel, I. (1978). Constructivism and teacher education. *The Elementary School Journal, 78*, 333–338.

Singer, D., & Singer, J. (2005). *Imagination and play in the electronic age*. Cambridge, MA: Harvard University Press.

Singer, D., Singer, J., D'Agostino, H., & DeLong, R. (2009). Children's pastimes and play in sixteen nations. *American Journal of Play, 1*(3), 283–312.

Skinner, E., & Belmont, M. (1993). Motivation in the classroom: Reciprocal effects of teacher behavior and student engagement across the school year. *Journal of Educational Psychology, 85*, 571–581.

Smith, K. (1993). Development of the primary teacher questionnaire. *Journal of Educational Research, 87*, 23–29.

Snow, K. (2007). Integrative views of the domain of child function: Unifying school readiness. In R. Pianta, M. Cox, & K. Snow (Eds.), *School readiness & the transition to kindergarten in the era of accountability* (pp. 197–216). Baltimore: Paul H. Brookes.

Sobel, D. (2008). *Childhood and nature: Design principles for educators*. Portland, ME: Stenhouse Publishers.

Stipek, D. (2002a). At what age should children enter kindergarten? A question for policy makers and parents. *SRCD Social Policy Report, 16*(2), 1–20.

Stipek, D. (2002b). *Motivation to learn: Integrating theory and practice, 4th edition*. Boston: Allyn & Bacon.

Stipek, D., & Byler, P. (1997). Early childhood education teachers: Do they practice what they preach? *Early Childhood Research Quarterly, 12*, 305–325.

Stipek, D., & Byler, P. (2004). The early childhood classroom observation measure. *Early Childhood Research Quarterly, 19*, 375–397.

Stipek, D., Feiler, R., Byler, P., Ryan, R., Milburn, S., & Salmon, J. (1998). Good beginnings: What difference does the program make in preparing young children for school? *Journal of Applied Developmental Psychology, 19*, 41–66.

Stipek, D., Feiler, R., Daniels, D., & Milburn, S. (1995). Effects of different instructional approaches on young children's achievement and motivation. *Child Development, 66*, 209–223.

Tharp, R., & Gallimore, R. (1988). Rousing minds to life: Teaching, learning, and schooling in social context. New York: Cambridge University Press.

Tobin, J., Hsueh, Y., & Karasawa, M. (2009). *Preschool in three cultures revisited*. Chicago: University of Chicago Press.

Valiente, C., Lemery-Chalfant, K., Swanson, J., & Reiser, M. (2008). Prediction of children's academic competence from their effortful control, relationships, and classroom participation. *Journal of Educational Psychology, 100*, 67–77.

Van Scoter, J., Ellis, D., & Railsback, J. (2001). *Technology in early childhood education: Finding the balance*. Retrieved from http://educationnorthwest.org/

Vecchiotti, S. (2003). Kindergarten: An overlooked educational policy priority. *SRCD Social Policy Report, 17*(2), 1–20.

Vygotsky, L. S. (1978). *Mind in society: The development of higher psychological processes*. Cambridge, MA: Harvard University Press.

Wang, C., & Hoot, J. (2006). Information and communication technology in early childhood education. *Early Education and Development, 17*, 317–322.

Wang, J., Elicker, J., McMullen, M., & Mao, S. (2008). Chinese and American preschool teachers' beliefs about early childhood curriculum. *Early Child Development and Care, 178*(3), 227–249.

Wartella, E., Caplovitz, A., & Lee, J. (2004). From Baby Einstein to Leapfrog, from Doom to The Sims, from instant messaging to internet chat rooms: Public interest in the role of interactive media in children's lives. *SRCD Social Policy Report, 18*(4), 3–19.

Webster-Stratton, C., Reid, M. J., & Hammond, M. (2004). Treating children with early-onset conduct problems: Intervention outcomes for parent, child, and teacher training. *Journal of Clinical Child and Adolescent Psychology, 33*, 105–124.

Weinstein, R. (2002). *Reaching higher: The power of expectations in schooling*. Cambridge, MA: Harvard University Press.

Weiss, H., Caspe, H., & Lopez, E. (2006). Family involvement in early childhood education. *Harvard Family Research Project, 1,* 1–8.

Wells, N. (2000). At home with nature: Effects of 'greenness' on children's cognitive functioning. *Environment and Behavior, 32,* 775–795.

Wells, N., & Evans, G. (2003). Nearby nature: A buffer of life stress among rural children. *Environment and Behavior, 35*(3), 311–330.

Wells, N., & Lekies, K. (2006). Nature and the life course: Pathways from childhood nature experiences to adult environmentalism. *Children, Youth and Environments, 16,* 1–24.

White, R. (2004). *Young children's relationship with nature: Its importance to children's development and the earth's future.* Retrieved from http://www.whitehutchinson.com/children/articles/childrennature.shtml

Wilkinson, L. C., & Silliman, E. R. (1997). Classroom language and literacy learning. *Handbook of Reading Research, 3*(21), 337–360.

Woodard, E., & Gridina, N. (2000). *Media in the home: The fifth annual survey of parents and children.* Philadelphia: The Annenberg Public Policy Center of the University of Pennsylvania.

Xue, Y., & Meisels, S. (2004). Early literacy instructions and learning in kindergarten: Evidence from the early childhood longitudinal study—kindergarten class of 1998–1999. *American Educational Research Journal, 41,* 191–229.

Yan, Z. (2006). What influences children's and adolescents' understanding of the complexity of the Internet? *Developmental Psychology, 42,* 418–428.

Zajac, R., & Hartup, W. (1997). Friends as coworkers: Research review and classroom implications. *The Elementary School Journal, 98,* 3–9.

Zigler, E., Gilliam, W., & Jones, S. (2006). *A vision for universal preschool education.* New York: Cambridge University Press.

Index

Adjustment, school. *See* Early school adjustment
Affection, 69
Age and school readiness, 35–36
Aggressive tendencies, children with, 52–54
American Psychological Association (APA), 60
  Center for Psychology in Schools and Education (CPSE), 69, 174
Anxiety, 131
Approaches to learning, 41–43
Assessment of Learner-Centered Practices (ALCP), 74–75
Attachment theory, 71
Attention problems, 45, 131
Attunement, 69

Balancing educational experiences, 135–136
Banking Time intervention, 72–73
Big Math for Little Kids, 178
Birch, S., 70
Blair, C., 37–38, 39, 43
Blatchford, P., 79–80
Bodrova, E., 96
Bowlby, John, 71
Bridging Cultures Project, 178
Butler, L., 82

Calvert, S., 119
Center for Research on Education, Diversity and Excellence (CREDE), 175

Center on the Social and Emotional Foundations for Early Learning (CSEFEL), 175
Chandler, M., 19
Child-centered approaches, 94, 109, 110 (figure)
Children
  with aggressive tendencies, 52–54
  approaches to learning in the classroom, 146–147
  changes from 5 to 7, 11–20
  changes in school contexts and, 20–23
  educational technology for, 118–128
  emotional regulation by, 39–41, 50 (table)
  executive function by, 37–39, 50 (table), 122
  with inhibited or withdrawn tendencies, 54–57, 150
  memory capacities and strategies, 13–15
  perspective-taking by, 18–19
  positive approaches to learning in the classroom, 41–43
  reasoning and logical thinking by, 16–18
  relationships with other children, 78–84, 154–157
  relationships with teachers, 69–77, 152–153
  responsible decision making by, 51 (table)

at risk for adjustment
    difficulties, 49–52
self-reflection by, 15–16
self-regulation by, 12–13, 36, 37,
    48–49, 148–149
typical ways of thinking and
    behaving in 5 to 7 shift of,
    23–24
views of school, 60–62
Children and Nature Network
    (C&NN), 176
Children's Digital Media Center,
    Georgetown University,
    119, 175
Classroom Assessment Scoring
    System (CLASS), 99
Classroom(s)
    assessment, 99
    climate, 99–101, 101–102 (table),
        162–163
    environment, 31–32
    instruction, 107–109, 166
    organization, 102–105, 106
        (table), 164–165
    promoting self-regulation in,
        50–51 (table)
    technology use in,
        115–117, 118 (figure)
Climate, classroom, 99–101,
    101–102 (table), 162–163
Cognitive processes, control of,
    37–39
Collaborative for Academic, Social,
    and Emotional Learning
    (CASEL), 69, 174
Comer, James, 68
Comer's School Development
    Program (SDP), 11, 74,
    176–177
Competence, social, 79, 83 (table)
Computers. See Technology
Concrete operations, 17–18
Connected knowing, 129
Constructive play, 98
Constructivist perspectives,
    95, 164–165
Contemporary teacher beliefs,
    26–27 (table), 144–145

Contexts, changes in school,
    20–23
Control of cognitive processes,
    37–39, 122
Control of emotional processes,
    39–41
Control of motivated behavior,
    41–43
Conversations, instructional, 96
Creativity, 131
Cristol, D., 126
Curiosity, 131

Decision making, responsible,
    51 (table)
Dependability, 69
Developmental shift from early to
    middle childhood, 11–12
    changes in school contexts,
        20–23
    changes in the child, 12–20
Dewey, J., 117
Digital divide, 117
Doherty, W., 96
Domains of readiness, 36–37
    approaches to learning and,
        41–43, 146–147
    emotional regulation (ER) in,
        39–41
    executive function (EF) in,
        37–39, 122
    profiles of school readiness and,
        43–45
Downer, J., 58
Duncan, G., 43, 45
Dynamic ecological model, 10–11

Early Childhood Classroom
    Observation Measure
    (ECCOM), 99
Early Childhood Environmental
    Rating Scale-Revised
    (ECERS-R), 99
Early Connections: Technology in
    Early Childhood Education,
    Northwest Educational
    Technology Consortium
    (NETC), 176

Early school adjustment
    associations with later school
        achievement, 43
    children at risk for adjustment
        difficulties, 49–52
    children with aggressive
        tendencies and, 52–54
    children with inhibited or
        withdrawn tendencies and,
        54–57, 150
    domains of readiness and, 36–43
    models, 33–35
    readiness of teachers and, 45–48
    readiness of the school and,
        57–60
Early to middle childhood
        developmental shift, 11–12
    changes in school context,
        20–23
    changes in the child, 12–20
Ecological perspective
    described, 9–11
    examples, 7–9
Effortful control (EC) processes, 38
Elias, M., 82
Elkind, D., 117, 127
Emotional regulation (ER), 39–41,
        50 (table)
Epstein, J., 84–86
Executive function (EF), 37–39,
        50 (table), 122

Family involvement, 65–67, 84–87,
        158–159
Family involvement Network of
        Educators (FINE),
        174–175
Five Standards, 97
5 to 7 developmental shift, 12
Focus and attention, 131

Gallimore, R., 96
Gardner, H., 129
Gender and school readiness,
        35–36
Gimbert, B., 126
Goal setting, 51 (table)
Greenfield, P., 127

Hamre, B. K., 102
Harter, S., 15
Herald-Brown, S., 78
Howes, C., 76
Hyson, M., 40

Incredible Years, The, 177–178
Informational Society for
        Technology in Education, 126
Inhibited or withdrawn
        tendencies, children with,
        54–57, 150
Instructional conversations, 96
Instructional formats, 104–105
Instructional strategies,
        107–109, 166
Intentional language
        stimulation, 108
Involvement, family, 65–67,
        84–87, 158–159
Izard, C., 53

Kellert, S., 128, 129
Knowing, connected, 129
Konold, T., 44, 45

Ladd, G., 70, 78
Lalonde, C., 19
Last Child in the Woods: Saving Our
        Children From Nature-Deficit
        Disorder, 128
Learner-centered principles, 25, 94,
        167–168
Learning
    approaches to, 41–43
    children's approaches to,
        146–147
    fostered with technology,
        124–126, 169–170
    playful, 105
    scientific, 131
    self-directed, 51 (table)
    social and emotional (SEL), 82
Learning Together: Children and
        Adults in a School
        Community, 104
Leong, D. J., 96
LoCasale-Crouch, J., 58

Logical thinking and reasoning, 16–18
Louv, R., 128

Management of classroom behavior, 104
Mashburn, A., 58
Memory capacities and strategies, 13–15
Mind, theories of, 18–19
Montessori, Maria, 46
Multimedia. *See* Technology

National Association for the Education of Young Children (NAEYC), 25, 32, 69, 173
National Education Goals Panel (NEGP), 57–60
Nature. *See* Outdoor education
Direct contact with, 128–129
Indirect contact with, 129
Vicarious contact with, 129
No Child Left Behind Act, 33, 141

Observational powers, 131
Olweus Bullying Prevention Program, 178
Organization, classroom, 102–105, 106 (table), 164–165
Outdoor education, 128–135, 171–172

Paley, V., 41, 81
Parents partnering with teachers, 65–67, 84–87, 158–161
Partnerships. *See* Relationships
PBS Teachers, 176
Pellegrini, A., 79–80
Perspectives, developmental
constructivist, 95, 164–165
ecological, 7–11
teachers', 24–25
Perspective-taking, 18–19
Physical activity, 131–132
Physical play, 98
Piaget, J., 97–98
Pianta, R., 11, 44, 45, 58, 71, 99, 102

Planning, 51 (table)
Play, 98–99
Playful learning, 105
Practices, classroom, 91–95, 109–112, 139–142
classroom climate and, 99–101, 101–102 (table)
classroom organization and, 102–105, 106 (table)
social-constructivist approaches to, 95–99
Preschool experience and school readiness, 35–36
children's views of schools and, 60–62
Pretend play, 98
Profiles of school readiness, 43–45
Prosocial programs, 119
Providing Alternative Thinking Strategies (PATHS), 177

Raver, C., 53
Readiness of teachers, 45–48
Reasoning and logical thinking, 16–18
Recess, 80–81
Reciprocal teaching, 107–108
Reform models, school, 67–69
Reiser, M., 78
Relationships
child-child, 78–84, 154–157
importance of fostering positive, 67–69, 87–89
between parents and teachers, 65–67
school reform models and, 67–69
teacher-child, 69–77, 152–153
teacher-parent, 65–67, 84–87, 158–161
working models of, 71
Responsible decision making, 51 (table)
Responsive Classroom, 177
Reticent behavior, 54
Rimm-Kaufman, S., 11, 47
Ritchie, S., 76

Scaffolding, 96
School, Family, and Community Partnerships: Your Handbook for Action, 85
School Development Program, 68
School readiness
  age, gender, and preschool experience effect on, 35–36
  approaches to learning and, 41–43
  classroom environment and, 31–33
  control of cognitive processes in, 37–39
  domains of, 36–45
  early school adjustment models and, 33–35
  profiles of, 43–45
  readiness of the school and, 57–60, 151
  of teachers, 45–48
School(s)
  children's views of, 60–62
  contexts changes, 20–23
  reform models, 67–69
Second Step, 177
Self-control, 37
Self-directed learning, 51 (table)
Self-reflection, 15–16
Self-regulation, 12–13, 36, 37
  emotional regulation (ER) and, 39–41
  fostering, 48–49, 148–149
Sesame Street, 119
Short-term memory, 13–15
Snow, K., 37
Social and emotional learning (SEL), 82
Social behavior, 51 (table)
Social competence, 79, 83 (table)
Social-constructivist approaches, 95–99
Social play, 98
Stipek, D., 35, 36, 76

Teacher Relationship Interview (TRI), 71
Teachers
  adapting practices to fit children's developmental needs, 91–95, 139–142
  contemporary and traditional beliefs about children's development and learning, 26–27 (table), 144–145
  fostering child-child relationships, 79–80
  perspectives on development and practice, 24–25
  qualities and classroom climate, 101–102 (table)
  readiness of, 45–48
  relationships with children, 69–77, 152–153
  relationships with parents, 65–67, 84–87, 158–161
  supporting emotional regulation, 41
Technology
  for children, 118–128
  fostering learning and development with, 124–126, 169–170
  portable, 123
  use in the classroom, 115–117, 118 (figure)
Tharp, R., 96
Theories of mind, 18–19
Thinking, logical, 16–18
Traditional teacher beliefs, 26–27 (table), 144–145

UCLA Center for Mental Health in Schools, 174
Vygotsky, L. S., 96

Weinstein, R., 60
Working models of relationships, 71

You Can't Say You Can't Play, 81

Zone of proximal development (ZPD), 96

CORWIN

A SAGE Company

The Corwin logo—a raven striding across an open book—represents the union of courage and learning. Corwin is committed to improving education for all learners by publishing books and other professional development resources for those serving the field of PreK–12 education. By providing practical, hands-on materials, Corwin continues to carry out the promise of its motto: **"Helping Educators Do Their Work Better."**